ESOTERICISM FOR EVERYONE

Interviews with Aldo La Fata

⊕

ESOTERICISM
FOR EVERYONE

Interviews with Aldo La Fata

⊕

Bruno Bérard
Aldo La Fata

🜨 Angelico Press

First published
by Angelico Press 2025
© Angelico Press 2025

For information, address:
Angelico Press
169 Monitor St.
Brooklyn, NY 11222
angelicopress.com

979-8-89280-122-5 (pbk)
979-8-89280-123-2 (cloth)

Cover design: Michael Schrauzer

Table of Contents

Preface

Esotericism has been around for millennia, if not since the dawn of mankind, as we have delved ever deeper into the mysteries of God, the world, and human life.

In the nineteenth century, esotericism and occultism—the "false twins" (J. P. Laurant)—reached such a paroxysm that both nouns appeared to designate them; it was René Guénon's work to distinguish them and codify esotericism.

Even today, in the midst of largely secularized Western cultures, modern esotericism continues to flourish: New Age, ufology, personal development, and so on.

Over the last few decades, a great deal of academic work has been carried out on all forms of esotericism, from ancestral megalithism to modern philosophical gnosticism. However, the historicist approach, which is descriptive by nature, needs to be complemented by assessments and value judgments, and we need to know from what point of view these judgments are being made.

Aldo La Fata, whose "cognitive humility" was so aptly described by Carlo Gambescia, and whose intimacy with Catholicism is neither occult or outrageously overt, offers the immense advantage of the kind of point of view sought for here.

Aldo La Fata's profound erudition is never cluttered with words and his manner of speaking is frank and clear, all of which strikes us as the best "touchstone" for dealing with esotericism. But let the reader be the judge.

To be clear: whereas one might speak of the metaphysical (science, doctrines...) whenever metaphysics is involved,

Aldo La Fata speaks to us in these conversations about esoterisms, whenever it is clearly the esoteric element that is
under consideration and is significant to him. The metaphysical or the esoteric are then as much paths as they are
the highest possible goal.

We will forget history then, historicist history at any rate,
as well as esotericism as such, and, in a case such as this, we
will perceive the presence of the esoteric hidden within the
world and in the human heart; further, we will perceive the
bond that unites them—and thereby the unity towards
which that bond points the way.

Bruno Bérard

Chapter 1

Esotericism and Science

When the term "esotericism" was coined in the 19th century,
all esoteric approaches—movements delving into the mysteries
of life, the world and God—were brought together under a
single term. If every esoteric approach could be called a science
in the etymological sense of knowledge, then the new notion of
esotericism is a science in the second degree. If we now ask how
this knowledge is to be organized, the further question imme-
diately arises of how to go beyond mere historical description.

Bruno Bérard (**BB**). These interviews will help us characterize what esotericism is, and the final one will offer a definition. But let's get started... Can you tell us a little about
this word and, as a first approach, what it means?

Esotericism or occultism

Aldo La Fata (**AF**). It's worth pointing out that, unlike the
adjective, which seems to have always existed, the noun is
very recent. It first appeared in German (*die Esoterik*) in
1792,[1] then in French in 1828,[2] before being used copiously

---

[1] Noted by Monika Neugebauer-Wölk in "Der Esoteriker und die
Esoterik...," *Aries Journal*, no. 2, 2010; in Johan Philipp Gabler's edition
of Johann Gottfried Eichhorn's *Urgeschichte*.

[2] Noted by Jean-Pierre Laurant, *L'Ésotérisme* (Paris: Cerf, 1993), 40–
41; in Jacques Matter, *Histoire critique du gnosticisme et de son influence*.

by Éliphas Lévi for example, often as an approximate replacement for *philosophia perennis* or *philosophia occulta.*[3]

BB: Hence the distinctions not always made between "esotericism" and "occultism," the latter term even used by a Robert Amadou, for example, until the end of the 20th century in the sense of "esotericism."

AF: However, this distinction was definitively established by René Guénon in the first half of the 20th century. It should be noted that the noun appeared and spread at the dawn of the secularization of culture in Europe. Such an appearance, i.e., the need to define, marks the moment of the eclipse of the obvious!

Esotericism and exotericism

BB: The etymology, as recalled by Jean Borella in particular, is also instructive.

AF: The Greek adjective *esoterikos* itself gives three indications. *Eso* means "inside," with an idea of movement: "towards the inside"; *ter* (from *teros*) indicates a comparison: "more towards the inside (than)"; and the ending *ikos* indicates a nuance of specificity: "that which has the particularity of going more towards the inside (than)." The word thus implies three key aspects: the notion of "interior" or deepening, which is also found in its Arabic equivalent *bâtin* (also "cavern," "matrix"); the notion of permanent movement towards the ever more interior, which refutes any "installed," fixed, definitive esotericism; and the notion of comparison: that is, the relative opposition between "esotericism" and "exotericism."

[3] Cf. Antoine Faivre, *Access to Western Esotericism* (Albany: State University of New York Press, 1994), 10.

4

BB: *Relative* opposition, as you say; no esotericism without exotericism, without support from a tradition, and no more absolute exotericism than absolute, pure esotericism, stripped of all form and liberated from all revelation (as Hegel would have wished, for example). But let's leave etymology for a more common definition of esotericism.

True and false esotericism

AF: At first glance, and in the most common sense of the term, "esotericism" refers to occult, secret, or hidden knowledge accessible only to the few. The term, with its Platonic and Aristotelian roots, actually referred to the oral teachings of the master, or even to some "material" that could only be consulted by Academy students. After twenty-five centuries, the term came to designate any spiritual orientation, rite, doctrine, or secret knowledge reserved for a privileged few.

Hence, clearly, the disquieting fascination it exerts above all on less culturally equipped and more imaginative minds, i.e., those not endowed with intellectually adequate tools of discernment. This also explains the great success of popularized or romanticized esotericism, especially among young people, who are generally its most casual users and followers, until middle age and the challenges of everyday life diminish their interest. In fact, it would not be wrong to speak of esotericism as a "literary genre" comparable to science fiction or so-called "escapist literature," the main purpose of which is for entertainment or as a pastime. With esoteric literature, the tastes of a certain class of readers attracted by the sensational, by anything out of the ordinary, are satisfied. As a friend of mine who understands these subjects has very well observed, this kind of literature

5

is often no more than a fascinating "playground for the mind."[4]

Of course, this doesn't mean it should be rejected; far from it. For, if there is fantasy and daydreaming, there is also the creative imagination, that is, the active imagination through which we can also grasp spiritual realities. Perhaps we'll talk more about this later, but in the meantime, let's start coming to grips with this concept, which I would say is a fundamental key to understanding authentic or traditional esotericism—that esotericism, just to be clear, which has an authentic spiritual basis and a history to be taken very seriously.

BB: Just reading how Antoine Faivre has listed gnosticism as well as theology, spiritism as well as gnosis as esoterisms it seems essential to distinguish, as you do, authentic esotericism from the others, but it is still necessary to specify what is meant by "authentic esotericism."

AF: To borrow an idea, I'd say that "authentic" esotericism would be akin to the so-called "hard sciences," which require rigor, study, and effort to be understood and then applied, whereas "pseudo" esotericism, or simply the literary, even the superficial, would be like the "soft sciences," which require neither adequate preparation nor effort to understand, let alone empirical demonstration. The adept then assiduously acquires and appropriates "knowledge," unfortunately based on uncertain elements, conjecture, and sometimes even fantasy. Some ecclesiastical scholars have

---

[4] Italian: *"parco giochi per la mente."* This definition is that of Turin-based researcher and scholar Dario Chioli (1956), who honors me with his friendship and whom I consider a great expert on the subject.

rightly spoken of *gnosi pura* ("pure gnosis") for esotericism of the first type, and *gnosi spuria* ("false gnosis") for esotericism of the second type—*spurio* meaning precisely counterfeit, falsified, false.

BB: But one should not for all that confuse esotericism with gnosis.

AF: Absolutely: gnosis (the moon) should not be confused with esotericism (the finger pointing to the moon). But apart from this necessary clarification, I believe that the ecclesiastical prejudice against a certain pseudo-esotericism is somewhat well-founded. Because, in fact, there has been a false esotericism reminiscent of, and in many ways related to, Gnosticism in the strict sense—i.e., that which flourished and developed in Alexandria, Egypt, and Rome, and whose doctrines are incompatible with those put forward by the Church of Rome, and by the very first Christian communities. This is a highly complex issue that would require countless clarifications and insights that I cannot even briefly address here. But I would like to make it clear that the esotericism considered false by the Church—and here I agree with her—is above all that which contrasts sharply with her "orthodoxy" and "orthopraxy."

BB: Can you give other examples of false esotericism or pseudo-esotericism?

AF: Yes. We could refer to all those who propose an *exclusivist* vision of reality, i.e., a sectarian and therefore heretical vision,[5] in open contrast to other visions or perspectives. In

[5] "Heresy" derives from the Greek αἵρεσις (*hairesis*) which in turn derives from the verb αἱρέω (*haireo*): "to seize," "to take," but also "to choose" or "to elect," and thus takes on an exclusivist meaning.

this sense, we could also go so far as to say that in its theories and methods even scientism is a form of "false esotericism," given that it goes so far as to attribute to the physical and experimental sciences the capacity to satisfy all human problems and needs—even spiritual ones. But false esotericism is also that which, as we say, "makes a hodge-podge of everything," i.e., indiscriminately brings together, without distinction, the most disparate doctrines and beliefs.

BB: A case in point?

AF: I'm thinking of the movement to which the mass media has given the name *New Age*. It's an umbrella term for a vast movement, a subculture, comprising numerous alternative psychological, social, and pseudo-spiritual currents. It emerged at the end of the 20th century in the Western world, and spread strongly first in the United States. Although some have seen these currents as something positive, or perhaps simply as harmless, there's no denying the alienation and dissociation from reality that have led many an individual, and entire families, to ruin their lives. Perhaps we can come back to this…

Having distanced ourselves from what authentic esotericism isn't or shouldn't be, we can begin to sketch out a more precise and definitive meaning, it being understood that in my opinion an absolute and scientific definition in the strict sense cannot be given.

Esotericism and esoterology

BB: Is there no legitimate scientific "esoterology"?

AF: Yes, of course. An historical-critical study of esotericism in all its forms is perfectly legitimate. The existence of serious, rigorous studies on the subject would be most welcome. But there is a risk that these studies will take over and that the spiritual meaning will end up being neglected and ultimately forgotten. History—historicism—is not only a conquest of the enlightened mind; it can, as Nietzsche reminded us, turn into a "devouring fever" and lead us to ruin. To archive and sift through esotericism in all its forms is to distort it, weaken it, impoverish it, reduce it to an exotic museum relic, and thus to something very different from what it really is. I therefore believe that a good esoterologist[6] must also be a good esotericist, just as a good theologian must also be an actual believer. For without a living relationship with the discipline studied, there can be no real acquisition and conquest. So, of course, those who stop at the limits of the demonstrable (esoterologists) will be less wrong than those who don't stop there (esotericists); but those who don't stop there (esotericists) will be more likely to go further. And "going beyond," I believe, is precisely the essence of esotericism, its office, and its true purpose.

Esoterologists and esotericists

BB: Wouldn't it be better to provide some bibliographical references?

AF: Certainly. In French, I'd suggest at least six titles, three by accredited esoterologists and three by equally accredited esotericists—as if to emphasize that we must always try to strike a balance between Science and Faith, so as not to fall

---

[6] This neologism is found in Émile Poulat, "Introduction to Jean-Pierre Brach & Jérôme Rousse-Lacordaire," *Études d'histoire de l'éso-térisme. Mélanges offerts à Jean-Pierre Laurant pour son soixante-dixième anniversaire* (Paris: Éditions du Cerf, 2007), 8.

into either scientism or fideism. So, on one side of the scale I'd put the now-classic *Qu'est-ce que l'ésotérisme?* by Pierre A. Riffard, *L'Ésotérisme* by Jean-Pierre Laurant, and *L'Ésotérisme* by Antoine Faivre; and on the other hand, Luc Benoist's *The Esoteric Path: An Introduction to the Hermetic Tradition*, Raymond Abellio's *La fin de l'ésotérisme*, and Frithjof Schuon's *Esoterism as Principle and as Way*. These are not very easy texts to read, but on the whole offer a fairly broad and, I'd say, serious overview of the subject, provided of course that some knowledge of the field is already established. And that's precisely the purpose of our conversations, to offer an introduction that facilitates access to other insights. We're trying here to provide an "esotericism within reach," an "esotericism for everyone."

BB: Which would make a good title for this book. Staying with the theme of "esotericism and science," there's not only the approach to a particular esotericism, which can range from a strictly scientific historical-critical approach to the most zealous and propagandistic panegyric or apology, there's also the fact that both "esotericism" and "science" refer to the notion of knowledge. How would you characterize each of these types of knowledge?

Esotericism and knowledge

AF: It's certainly a decisive question that can't be avoided. In fact, it's no coincidence that I referred to scientism as a form of pseudo-esotericism. If there is a relationship between false esotericism and scientism, or between a false path and a false science, it's clear that there must also be one between true science and true esotericism.

BB: In what way?

AF: As you rightly say, both refer to the notion of knowledge, but it is a matter of human knowledge in the case of science, and of spiritual or divine knowledge in the case of esotericism. The term "knowledge," which derives from the Latin "cognoscere,"[7] can take on different meanings depending on the context in which it is used, but it is to some extent related to the concept of information. However, knowledge cannot and must not be confused with semantics. We say that knowledge presupposes a certain form of identification with the known object, which, in the case of information, is to be excluded.

BB: To what extent, then, can science be said to possess or aspire to knowledge?

AF: We could answer insofar as it succeeds (*quodammodo* as St. Thomas Aquinas would say, that is, "in a certain way") in making conceptual acquisitions coincide with empirical verifications. Here, too, the question would require a lengthy explanation that we cannot enter into here—but then, there are entire treatises on this subject. In short, at issue is the distinction we made at the beginning: when is true knowledge acquired, and should it be sufficient for us?—the answer to which is that true knowledge occurs when the subject and the known object become identified, become one.

BB: Of course. But this identification needs to be clarified. Does it mean that the subject fades into the object, or that the object fades into the subject?

---

[7] Derived from *cum*: "with" and *gnoscere*: "to know, to cognize" the latter from an Indo-European root related to Ancient Greek γιγνώσκω (*gignosko*). The addition of "with" indicates that "cognizance" is appropriated, internalized knowing, whereas mere "knowing" remains external.

AF: Here, too, we could evoke the many answers that have come to us from the philosophy and doctrines of the world's various religious traditions (when they have produced speculations of a theoretical nature). Esotericism, however, is not a gnoseology (i.e., not a theory of knowledge) and, since it is not a philosophy either, it can be said that it is not interested in a theoretical answer, which is always left in the background. Like science, it is not interested in particular objects, but in the absolute object, that is, the root and source of all objects. So: not the particular, but the universal—this is its principal quest. What's more, esotericism doesn't pursue knowledge through the mind or reflexive reason, following the appropriate means and methods, but through "the light of the intellect" (Dante), that faculty which presides over and also transcends the mental and cognitive faculties. For esotericism, it is not the thinker and the thought that must become alike (a misunderstood Platonic suggestion); rather, both must be transcended into the divine. In conclusion, and if you agree, we could further simplify matters by saying that esotericism is concerned with transcendence, whereas science is concerned with immanence.

BB: This makes a good segue into our interview on "esotericism and religion."

Chapter 2

Esotericism and Religion

A great specialist like Antoine Faivre seems to lump all esotericism under the same banner, be it theology or heretical gnosticism, or areligious esotericism. What, then, is the relationship between esotericism and religion?

BB: According to the groupings made by specialists, esotericism within religions includes both theologies and nondenominational approaches. How would you characterize the links between esotericism and religion?

Esotericism: theory or path?

AF: I understand the analytical need of science, with its distinctions and classifications, but this approach doesn't work for esotericism if we accept that it is a "way" and not a theory, a system of ideas, or a doctrine as such. Theories and doctrines may be a starting point, but they are not the "way." Not to mention that we're not dealing with a single path. When we talk about esotericism, then, we must avoid listing everything under the same heading or term. In my opinion, enumerations do not bring clarification, but most often betray an intention.

BB: What intention do you mean?

AF: That of transforming a spiritual question into a theory or idea subservient to one's own point of view, or into a closed system with a constrained outcome. Which can

13

oblige us to change our mind and reformulate everything all over again. Sometimes, we fall so in love with our idea that it becomes impossible to do without it—to the detriment of the truth. This tendency to explain and pigeonhole everything should be avoided when talking about esotericism.

BB: Can you give a few examples?

AF: Of course! I'm talking about the very modern tendency to enclose what is not understood in elaborate conceptual categories (especially historical, sociological, and psychological) which, in reality, not only explain nothing, but sometimes even touch upon the grotesque. Think of Umberto Eco's *Foucault's Pendulum* (1988). It's a novel, all right, but there's a teasing and demystifying intention towards esotericism, all too confounded with modern "conspiracy theories," among other things. Naturally, Eco distinguished quite well between true and false esotericism (in that sense, he was an expert), and it's just as likely that his book was really intended to help us distinguish one from the other—but the impression the non-expert reader gets is quite different, and one finishes the last page and closes the book thinking: "so, it was all a joke!"

BB: Another example?

AF: Such is the case of Antoine Faivre (1934–1921), who also has great merits in "formal" esotericism. Among other things, in a way, he was himself an "esoterist," a Christian esoterist and a Freemason (belonging to the Grande Loge Nationale de France). Well, in his studies, Faivre has given esotericism a unique interpretation, adhering to certain schemas and criticizing others. For example, his criticism of René Guénon or his sympathy for the Estonian-Russian esotericist Valentin Tomberg are well known. In any case, to lump all forms of esotericism together in a single cauldron would be a mistake. Occultism, esotericism, and magic, thank God, are not the same thing, and it would be a serious mistake to pass them off as such.

BB: That's a clarification I can live with. But back to the question of the link between esotericism and religion.

Esoteric or religious?

AF: (laughs) Indeed, it was almost a digression, but in the end it all ties in, in the sense that on the one hand I want to underscore a certain discontinuity, as historians and sociologists should do, and on the other to underscore common elements, as do those who don't have to hide their spirituality.

Yet it's true that there should be a difference and distance between religion and esotericism: religion is for everyone, while esotericism is for the few. There's no doubt about that. But the problem is whether it's possible to move from one to the other, or whether the two paths can converge, or even overlap. According to the greatest esotericist of the 20th century, René Guénon (1886–1951) whom, as you know, I greatly respect, exotericism (religion) and esotericism (primordial tradition) are complementary but substantially different paths. Moreover, according to Guénon, esotericism is not to be thought of as the "inner" part of religion, although it is true that esotericism develops and completes what religion may perhaps reveal only in a vague or simplified form.

BB: And do you agree with Guénon's distinction between exotericism and esotericism?

AF: In part, yes. I say only in part, because his discourse can indeed be applied to certain religions—I'm thinking of Islam and Judaism in particular—but, in an absolute sense, only to these (we'll come back to this when we tackle the discourse on the various esotericisms in the different religions) and certainly not to Christianity, which in fact doesn't seem to have envisaged this distinction (even if not all scholars agree on this). As you know, there are some serious scholars who believe there was such a thing as Christian esotericism, and others, just as serious, who claim the opposite. And then there are still others who take an intermediate position. Hard to understand, but it's worth a try!

BB: We can come back to this when we tackle the subject of Christian esotericism. For now, let's stick to the relationship between religion and esotericism...

AF: Of course! To understand the kind of relationship that can exist between religion and esotericism, we must first try to understand what religion is. Religion presupposes first and foremost faith (what I believe), while esotericism implies above all knowledge (what can be known, and what is veiled). But this would be a superficial way of looking at things, for in reality true faith is not belief, and knowledge is not simply what we know.

BB: This is certainly a misunderstanding upon which even the so-called "religious sciences" have stumbled. I'm thinking, for example, of Mircea Eliade's famous *A History of Religious Ideas*. His is a language that betrays an Enlightenment matrix.

AF: I couldn't agree more! "More than ever, everything in it seems simple and luminous, too simple and too luminous

16

perhaps," it was said, as soon as the first volume appeared.[1] I would add that Christians themselves, reasoning along these lines, would end up admitting that their faith is nothing but nonsense. This is a misunderstanding of Tertullian's *credo quia absurdum* ("I believe because it is absurd"),[2] which was uttered polemically against the Docetists, only to affirm the exact opposite afterwards: that the apostles' faith was not at all groundless nonsense, but something based on very concrete and real events they had witnessed. A similar argument could be made for esotericism. Indeed, if esotericism were simply knowledge, it could be learned in the same way as any school or university subject.

BB: Which is indeed the case in historical-critical approaches to our cognitive faculties, but that's why you speak of esotericism not as knowledge, but as a way.

AF: Absolutely! But religion is also a path, a path that requires faith. And what is faith? Absolute conviction in the truth and accuracy of an hypothesis? Undoubtedly. But secondarily and as a consequence of the main fact. The main fact is that faith presupposes grace. In the Gospels and, if I'm not mistaken, in the Acts of the Apostles, it is clearly stated that faith in Christ is one of the effects of God's

---

[1] Jean-Paul Roux, "M. Eliade. Histoire des croyances et des idées religieuses," tome I, in *Revue de l'histoire des religions*, tome 193, no. 2, 1978, 226–27.

[2] *Credibile est quia ineptum est. Et sepultus resurrexit; certum est quia impossibile* (We must believe it because it is absurd. He was buried, he is risen: that is certain since this is impossible); Tertullian, *De Carne Christi*, 5, 5 (Fr. trans. J.-P. Mahé, *La chair du Christ* [Paris: Cerf, 1975]).

grace, His gift.[3] So, we believe as a consequence of a spiritual fact. In the same way I would say that at the very basis of esotericism there is, so to speak, a spiritual fact. Perhaps the "spiritual fact" is the same, but the people who experience or receive it are different.

BB: In what sense "different"?

AF: I mean with a different mindset and a different vocation. So we shouldn't make it a question of superiority, or worse, of aspiring to superiority. In my opinion there are in this sense no privileged men. Privileges simply belong to the favorable conditions in which a person lives. *We are all beggars.* There's the wise man and there's the fool, but the situation can always be reversed. And this shows that we start from a common base.

Esotericism and grace

BB: Are you saying that, where some people benefit from the grace of a revelation and espouse a religious denomination, others, benefiting from a grace of another kind, will immerse themselves in esotericism?

AF: In reality, we don't know precisely whether it's a grace of "another order" or a special grace (what theologians call "sanctifying grace"), or whether it's the same grace but with different results—all of which effects are due to the diversity of the recipient's merits. The Latins used to say *cuique*

[3] "Then, as he wanted to go to Achaia, the brothers encouraged him and wrote to the disciples to welcome him. When he arrived there, he was a great help to those who had believed *by the grace of God*, for with great vigor he publicly refuted the Jews, demonstrating by the Scriptures that Jesus is the Christ" (Acts 18:27).

suum, "to each his own,"[4] and the Old Testament speaks of those who "found grace before God": Noah, Moses, David, etc.[5] But let's be clear. There's nothing automatic about "grace" in the Christian sense: some men seem to be favored by it, others not. But here we enter into a truly mysterious dynamic about which little can be said.

BB: Can we really speak of a "sanctifying grace" granted to those with an esoteric vocation?

AF: The discourse on grace from a theological point of view is, as you know, very complex. Thousands of pages have been written on the subject, and we can't get through it in a few words. Among other things, I'd like to avoid venturing assumptions or making the Magisterium say things it has never said, or would never say.

Esoteric language, religious language

BB: That's wise, but since we're talking about the relationship between religion and esotericism, aren't there a few parallels to be drawn, precisely in order to clarify the terms of the question?

AF: It's possible! So let's start by saying that esotericism speaks a different language than religion. I don't know whether or not there exists in French a text that gathers up esoteric terminology. If there isn't, I think it should be written, and present a summary of the most important esoteric concepts.

BB: As of 2013, there is a large dictionary in French cover-

---

[4] Derived from *suum cuique tribuere* in Roman law, meaning "to give to each his due."

[5] Noah, Genesis 6:8; Moses, Exodus 33:12–17; David, 2 Samuel 15:25.

ing esotericism—from the aborigines of Australia to ancient Scandinavia, from the Celts to Pharaonic Egypt, from early Christianity to Mesopotamian cuneiform, from Mesoamerica to Judaism, from Islam to India...[6]

AF: In Italy a work of this type was sketched out by the Christian hermeticist Paolo Virio (born Paolo Marchetti, 1910–1969) under the title *Lessico esoterico comparativo* [*Comparative Esoteric Lexicon*],[7] but is nowhere to be found. It was still only a fragmentary first draft, nothing that could be compared to a real dictionary.

BB: What role do you see for such a dictionary?

AF: First and foremost, to avoid the many misunderstandings that arise when talking about esotericism. Precise, shared definitions—wherever possible—could have prevented many misinterpretations and misunderstandings, even among the best-informed researchers. The usefulness of such a book, to give just one example, was recognized and acclaimed by many readers of Eco's *Foucault's Pendulum*, and then, a few years after its publishing success, someone actually wrote it.[8] But such a work, carried out according to the rules of the art, would in fact require a great deal of skill, perhaps too much, and so I suspect we'll have to wait several more years before seeing one. Maybe AI will write it, who knows! (laughs).

---

[6] Jean Servier (dir), *Dictionnaire de l'ésotérisme* (Paris: PUF, 2013), 1464 pages.

[7] Rome: Sophia Editions, 1971.

[8] Luigi Bauco, Francesco Millocca, *Dizionario del pendolo di Foucault*, a cura di Luciano Turrini (dir); (Ferrara: Gabriele Corbo Editore, 1989).

Grace and initiatory transmission

BB: Let's try, if you like, to give an example of a comparison between religious language and esoteric language. Staying with the previous theme, do you think there's an esoteric concept comparable to the concept of grace?

AF: By way of analogy, I would equate grace with initiatory transmission proper, i.e., the transmission of spiritual influence which, in Guénon's words, "allows the individual to order and develop those possibilities he carries with himself."[9]

BB: But this is transmitted through a chain of initiation and by men entrusted with the task, whereas in Christianity, grace is a free gift from God infused into the human soul by the Holy Spirit. How can there be any similarity?

AF: It is in human mediation, as in the case of the seven sacraments, which are given by human mediators. In this case, we speak precisely of "sacramental grace." The modes of transmission change, and the "facilitators" are different: consecrated men in the case of religion; spiritual masters in the case of esotericism.

BB: Certainly, and likewise, both ecclesiastical tradition and the Gospels (according to St Matthew, St Mark, St Luke and St John) are indeed human mediations, but true grace, the grace of faith, is without human intermediaries, isn't it?

AF: Of course, faith as an "inner grace," and in its supernatural nature has no intermediaries (apart, that is, from sacramental initiations), and certainly an esotericist, irre-

[9] *Perspectives on Initiation* (Ghent, NY: Sophia Perennis, 2002), 27.

spective of the initiation received from a spiritual master, must also possess it. I would even add that the grace of faith must be superabundant in the esotericist.

BB: Anything else you'd like to clarify about the distinction between religion and esotericism?

Religious esotericism, esoteric religion

AF: In general, I'd say that anything of a religious nature comes down to esotericism, and that anything of an esoteric nature comes down to religion. After all, it's man's relationship with the sacred or with God or with the transcendent that we're talking about. Except that, in the case of religion, we're talking about a relationship of fidelity, devotion, adoration, and veneration, whereas in the case of esotericism we're talking about something even more intimate and, I'd say, more profound, having to do with the potential development of all the possibilities latent in man—possibilities and potentials that bring together the physical, the psychic, and the spiritual. Religion doesn't exclude them (I'm thinking, for example, of the fulfillment of the so-called virtues of perfection, or cardinal virtues, which also have to do with the discipline of body and mind), but recommends them as an *ad extra habitus*, whereas esotericism, so to speak, obtains them, i.e., completes them from within, *ab intra*.

BB: So you mean that in religion we express ourselves in terms of exteriority, whereas in esotericism we express ourselves in terms of interiority?

AF: Well, yes, in a certain sense that's true, and I'd even say quite clearly so. Otherwise, we wouldn't be talking about a "morality of obedience," sexual morality, or a "morality of the virtues"; and Christians wouldn't be confusing Christian perfection with morality, or with the morality of servants and slaves, as Nietzsche interprets it. These confusions and distorting simplifications are not to be found in esotericism, which in many respects is also more rigorous in its language.

BB: We're still talking about real esoterism, aren't we?

AF: Of course we are! A "false" esoterism is, from the point of view of language, quite baffling.

BB: How would you conclude this interview on the relationship between religion and esotericism?

AF: I'll conclude by saying that religion and esotericism are not only interdependent, but complementary and necessary to each other, and in fact cannot exist separately. And I would add that the means may be different, but the goal is the same. In my opinion, the goal can only be the same, even though the means to achieve it may differ for each of us, and even though our individual aspirations and possibilities differ so much from one another. An esotericist may think that Paradise "is yet a prison" (as some Sufis have said), while any other ("exoterist") believer might deem this too ambitious a goal. In the end, however, neither of us knows the outcome of the journey, which is transcendent and therefore beyond all personal ideas and beliefs. I'll limit myself here to recalling the Gospel maxim: "Blessed are the last, for they shall be first."[10] Among other things, this also means that, in the afterlife, hierarchies are reversed.[11]

---

[10] Matt. 20:1.

[11] See Bruno Bérard, Aldo La Fata, *Paroles chrétiennes, contresens et vérités* (Editions L'Harmattan, 2025).

BB: Can we say, then, that in the afterlife "simple" men of faith can have a better or higher destiny than members of initiatic organizations?

AF: It's certainly possible, but, of course, who could say for sure? Nevertheless, I'd make a suggestion to those with esoteric aspirations: don't get caught up in any ideas of becoming "world champion"; it's better—to use a soccer metaphor—to keep a low profile, stay at the bottom of the standings.

Chapter 3
Esoteric Biography

An interest in esotericism is more than just intellectual curiosity. As "transforming knowledge," esotericism implies a personal approach, rooted in the life of the person who pursues it. To paraphrase Heidegger, every esoteric question implies the esoterist who asks it. Aldo La Fata is asked here about the most personal and intimate origins of his interest in these fields.

BB: Are your esoteric interests necessarily rooted in your life? Can you say a few words about that?

AF: I'd rather not talk about myself, but I understand that it contributes to the purpose of this book and deserves an effort.

BB: Yes, it can enlighten many readers, I think, by giving that personal touch to the subject. When did your interest in esotericism begin?

Julius Evola

AF: Now that I'm sixty, the memory of that moment is lost in the mists of time! (laughs). On a more serious note, I owe my discovery of esotericism to a few books by Julius Evola (1898–1974) found in my father's library. I was about twelve, but already thirsty for knowledge. I remember that Evola's books struck me, struck me not only for their content—weird and unusual to say the least—but also for their writing style, which I found truly engaging. Just think, after reading *Sintesi di dottrina della razza* (1941, "*Synthesis of the doctrine of race*") and *Il mito del sangue* (1941, "*The Myth of Blood*"), I told my father that I found this author more intelligent and profound than Jesus (laughs).

BB: I can imagine your father's perplexity!

Father director of Catholic Action and Franciscan Tertiary

AF: To say the least! (laughs). He was so taken aback that from then on he started passing me books on Christian catechetics and theology. At the time, my father was director of *Azione Cattolica Italiana*[1] (Catholic Action) and a Franciscan tertiary. So he was very committed, at home as well, to giving his children as Christian an education as possible. He must have done a good job with me since, in fact, when I became an adult, I always remained firmly rooted in Christianity. However, Evola greatly broadened my horizons and helped me to see my religion in a non-conformist way, and to respect others' religion as well as my own.

BB: And when does esotericism come into play?

René Guénon

AF: Esotericism really came into play in the seventies, through the work of René Guénon, whom I came to know through Evola. He quoted Guénon frequently and always

[1] The origins of *Azione Cattolica Italiana* date back to September 1867, when two young Italian academics, Mario Fani and Giovanni Acquaderni founded, in Bologna, the *Società della Gioventù Cattolica Italiana*, whose fundamental principles were obedience to the Pope, an educational project based on the study of religion, a life according to the principles of Christianity, and a deep commitment to charity towards the weakest and poorest.

with reverence, as if he were someone who knew and understood more than Evola did himself.

BB: I imagine you've read Guénon's books?

AF: Indeed, *Symboles de la Science sacrée* (posthumous collection, Gallimard, 1962) came out in Italian in 1975 (ed. *Il ramo d'oro*) and I bought it; I was sixteen. It was a real shock! I remember staying up two nights in a row to finish reading it.

BB: What impressed you most about this reading?

AF: The multiplicity of meanings enclosed in a symbol and the connection between symbols from all religions reinforced in me the idea of a unitary, universal divine plan and purpose.

BB: And esotericism as such?

AF: Before posing the problem of "esoteric organizations," it was the idea of esotericism as a linking system between all traditions that came to me. Reading Guénon's other works, which I finished later, perhaps when I was twenty-two or twenty-three, I got the idea of esotericism as something absolutely different from religion, even if the latter remains indispensable. In short, I adhered intellectually to the Guénonian "schema," which I found convincing, logical, and true.

BB: It wasn't without consequences, was it?

Roman esoteric circles

AF: The first was to feel the need for "regular" initiation. I began to frequent certain Roman "esoteric" circles (neo-Templars and "Rosicrucians" in particular), until I came across a singular character who, in that milieu, was nicknamed "the Doctor." He was a highly cultured man, as well as a recognized specialist in parapsychology, who at the time had been commissioned by the Church to study the Catholic mystic Maria Valtorta.[2] I was fascinated by this man, by his character, by the immensity of his knowledge, by his persuasive and refined discourse. He was a kind of Socrates who was only interested in the truth, and whose answers were always ready.

BB: I can see why he fascinated you...

AF: Yes, that was the case. I thought he was the master who would give me the initiation I so desired. However, he later revealed to me that he belonged to the school of Giuliano Kremmerz.[3] I must say that this news caused me more than a few perplexities, especially as this author had a reputation as a magician, whereas the idea of an esotericism linked to the Catholic religion had already crystallized for me.

BB: And how did it end?

AF: It was finally, after a series of rather unpleasant circumstances, that I distanced myself from this gentleman. But let's be clear: what I learned from him, and what he gave me in human terms too, I've never forgotten, and he cer-

---

[2] Caserta, March 14, 1897–Viareggio, October 12, 1961. Valtorta said she heard a "voice" she attributed to Jesus who prompted her to write, as if under dictation. The texts are now collected in the ten-volume work *L'Evangelo come mi è stato rivelato* ("The Gospel as it was revealed to me," published by Centro Editoriale Valtortiano, 1979). Her writings were placed on the index (1959), and Cardinal Joseph Ratzinger (as Prefect of the Congregation for the Doctrine of the Faith) twice confirmed the Magisterium's negative opinion (1985, 1988).

[3] Born Ciro Formisano (Portici, April 8, 1861–Beausoleil, May 7, 1930).

tainly played a central role in my life, for better or for worse! For better, because it helped me to get to know myself better in every sense of the word; for worse, because for a time it distanced me from my family and somewhat upset my human relationships.

BB: So, in the end, your experience of esotericism wasn't all that positive.

AF: Of course, but in terms of false or pseudo-esotericism, the real thing is quite different. Through this experience, I forged links with certain "anti-traditional" circles, to use Guénon's expression, but I was twenty-four!

BB: And what happened next?

Silvano Panunzio

AF: As the "magico-esoteric" parenthesis drew to a close, I became acquainted with the books of a certain Silvano Panunzio.[4] In Evolian circles, he was spoken of as a qualified and erudite Christian esotericist. I simply looked up his telephone number in the phone book and found it without difficulty; in those days, there was no *chat*, no social networks, and none of the multitude of diverse communications on the Internet that we know today. I didn't hesitate to give him a call, and I must say I was immediately won over by his exquisite kindness. He was a Catholic

---

[4] Born in Ferrara on May 16, 1918 and died in Pescara on June 10, 2010, Panunzio was the son of the famous legal philosopher and revolutionary syndicalist Sergio Panunzio. He was the author of numerous works, some of which have been translated into French and now feature in the L'Harmattan catalog: *Métaphysique de l'Évangile éternel* (2022) and *Propos sur René Guénon, Julius Evola, Frithjof Schuon et quelques autres* (2023).

and very knowledgeable about "esoteric" literature. Importantly, he didn't pretend to be a teacher and, indeed, he was a rather shy person.

BB: Would you say he was just a student of esoteric things or a "true esotericist"?

AF: I'd say both, all together. Savant and erudite, he certainly was, but without the pedantic attitude so typical of this milieu. He didn't feel superior to others, but he was very determined and totally focused on his goal.

BB: What was it?

AF: I would say: the search for God or the Absolute. All his mental and spiritual energies were channeled in this direction.

BB: Without getting into the subject of Christian esotericism, which we'll cover in a later interview, could you explain in what sense Panunzio can be considered a "Christian esotericist"?

AF: I would say both in the generic sense of a Christian student of esoteric doctrines and in the particular sense of a Christian imbued with these doctrines. In other words, I'm talking about a search that was not only intellectual, but also spiritual, and that included both the study of other religions (the search for *semina Verbi*: seeds of the Word outside Christianity), the constant reflection on universal symbols, and the quest—not just speculative—for an understanding of the mysteries of nature and the cosmos.

BB: Do you know if Panunzio was affiliated with an "esoteric" organization?

L'Alleanza Trascendente Michele Arcangelo

AF: I don't think so, although I can't say with absolute certainty. In fact, he never mentioned it to me. Officially, he was a Knight of the Order of Saints Maurice and Lazarus and, with others, had created an esoteric brotherhood under the name of *Alleanza Trascendente Michele Arcangelo* (Transcendent Alliance of Michael the Archangel).

BB: Were you part of it?

AF: Of course I was!

BB: What did it involve?

AF: It was a kind of new chivalric order, inspired by the highest ideals of the ancient chivalric orders of medieval Christendom. To put it simply, it was a kind of neo-Templarism, but without cloaks and daggers, without ceremonies, and without any kind of external pomp and circumstance. The acronym ATMA deliberately takes its name from the Sanskrit word *atma*, meaning the spiritual, transcendent Self. The purpose of this small organization, which never counted more than a dozen members (an esoterically non-random number), was to offer Christians seeking an initiation into esotericism a valid alternative to the many false initiations dispensed mainly by occultists.

BB: Which organizations in particular do you have in mind?

AF: Martinism, neo-Rosicrucians, Anthroposophy, but also other lesser-known organizations claiming alleged links with alchemy, Christian hermeticism, the Templars, etc.

BB: Were initiations given at ATMA?

AF: No, no, please! (laughs). Panunzio was a serious person! (laughs). Those who joined ATMA had only a few duties to fulfill, the first of which was always to remain faithful to the Church and its teachings. The main objective was to personify, preserve, and defend a transcendent and aristocratic conception of life, and to develop a sacred and symbolic dimension in the field of knowledge.

BB: So it was first and foremost on-the-job training?

AF: I'd say yes! The work of formation was both intellectual and moral, doctrinal and spiritual. Membership in the Alliance implied intimate observance of five "fundamental dispositions": prayer, diligence, study, discipline, and sacrifice.

BB: Prayer is very clear, but can you give some examples of the other four provisions?

AF: Diligence consisted essentially in never being idle, being dynamic, and organizing one's life in such a way as never to leave too many "empty spaces." In short, life had to be organized like that of a monk, alternating study, work, sport, and prayer.

BB: No free time?

AF: Yes, of course, but it was to be used for socializing, playing or listening to music, etc., in short, anything that might be a relief for the soul and a relaxation for the mind. Studies were to include the "sacred sciences" (theology, mysticism, metaphysics, symbolism, spirituality) and the "soft arts" (literature, cinema, music, painting), so as to develop a certain balance of knowledge as well. In short, there should be no gaps in intellectual training, nor any form of monoideism.

BB: Which way?

AF: In the sense that we shouldn't concentrate too much on one idea, even if it's a spiritual one, but train the mind to be elastic and to understand everything as much as possible without fanaticism or fixations.

BB: One can certainly understand why. And what was meant by "discipline"?

AF: It was, on the one hand, fidelity to the principles of the Alliance and, on the other, obedience to the voices of the soul or conscience, or rather of our "spiritual guardian" (guardian angel) who, if we know how to listen with the right inner disposition, always leads us to just and virtuous action.

Finally, sacrifice is the most difficult part: abandoning the vanities and clamors of the world for the witness of truth and supreme love for Christ.

BB: A very noble observance! And was there anything else followers were required to do?

The sacred Gargano cave

AF: Yes, a special devotion to Archangel Michael. The commitment to respect the five fundamental dispositions was to be made at Monte Sant'Angelo, in Puglia, in the sacred grotto of Gargano, during the equivalent of a "vigil prior to knighthood." The initiation would have been given by the Archangel himself, without human mediation. But let's be clear: such a charismatic experience shouldn't suggest anything phantasmagorical or bordering on the fantastic with apparitions of angels, swords, or the Holy Grail. We're talking here, in the somewhat solemn setting of the grotto, about an experience that is intimate and incommunicable, but absolutely real. It may not have been systematically transmitted, but Panunzio lived it personally. And nobody in the world can assess the validity of this experience, not even me, who was part of it.

BB: And me even less, of course, but I'd be interested to know if this idea has any basis in esoteric literature.

AF: I'd say there's more than one, starting with the very rich literature on angelology, which finds confirmation in all Eastern and Western traditions. Guénon himself, who knew these things well, spoke of an "archangelic initiation" as being the prerogative of certain solitaries and inspired people, but absolutely real and traditional. Perhaps we'll come back to this later.

BB: To conclude this part of our interview, is there anything else you'd like to add?

AF: No, perhaps I've already said too much (laughs) and we could stop there.

BB: Just one last question, then: between then and now, what's been your path and where do you stand with esotericism?

AF: That's two questions (laughs)! Let's just say that I've tried to model my life on the principles of ATMA, and I still do. Panunzio said of me that I was "faithful and firm" (*fidus et firmus* in Latin), and in fact these two adjectives express my character and way of being: in my soul, I'm a soldier who would never abandon his guard. I just hope it's a virtue and not a flaw (laughs). Esotericism, in my research and in my life path, is always there, let's say in the background. After all, esotericism has taught me to discern, to open up vertical paths, and to breathe deeply. And then I'd say it's also an intellectual stimulant—and sometimes even an entertainment—this magmatic substance from which so many good things can come. I hope to be able to demonstrate this in our further conversations.

Chapter 4

A History of Esotericism

With a long history that can be imagined as far back as the origins of mankind, it could be said that esotericism, as such, is ahistorical. However, from ancestral megalithism to modern Gnosticism, esotericism has taken many different forms in different eras, and as such we can speak of a history of esotericism.

BB: Is esotericism, as such, ahistorical? On the other hand, certain currents have appeared at certain moments in history. Can you give us an overview?

Ahistorical esotericism

AF: Indeed, esotericism as a historical entity doesn't exist and never has, but a history of its many expressions, formulations, actualizations, and adaptations is certainly possible. However, it is more than a history of men, or rather souls, who have realized the possibility, sometimes within a religious and civil institutional framework and other times outside it.

BB: What do you mean by that?

AF: When we talk about esotericism, we're talking about a "culture of the soul" that answers to man's needs, needs that are both speculative and spiritual, but I'd say especially spiritual. We call "esotericism" a possible response, one among many, and therefore not the only one! There is a plurality of voices that answer to this "need," and they are never all the same: some are disjointed stammerings, others unfinished discourses, still others rigorous dialectics. Everything depends on the human subject making the statement. When it comes to esotericism, we can certainly speak of currents, or rather karst rivers from which springs emerge from time to time, here and there. It's the "history" of these springs that we can talk about, not the river that gave rise to them.

BB: What name would you give to this "underground river"?

AF: We cannot and must not speak of this solemn and grandiose "river," swollen with "crystal-clear" waters, because it springs, as that pre-eminent esoteric book of Christianity, the Apocalypse, reminds us, "from the throne of God and of the Lamb." (Apoc. 22:1)

BB: This is all very enigmatic (laughs)…

AF: Of course, but I can't talk about something mysterious by depriving it of mystery, as that would be like distorting it or turning it into something of little interest. However, it's no coincidence that I've chosen water and the "Throne" as symbols of Jewish and Christian thought. Better than others, they are undoubtedly the symbols with the most marked metaphorical vocation, and therefore the most apt to symbolize esotericism.

BB: How do they do this?

AF: One represents fluid, elusive mobility, the other stability and permanence: "the throne of the kings of Israel is established before the Lord for ever." (Book of 1st Kings, 2:45) Fluidity and immutability are, paradoxically perhaps, the two "intrinsic qualities" of esotericism.

BB: That's very convincing, but let's get back to the "story" of esotericism.

AF: Yes, that's the difficulty with esotericism, which is a kind of *summa summarum* (a sum of sums), but whose diversity can refer to any theme and all possible levels.

Esotericism, a human story

As I was saying, esotericism is first and foremost the story of men, special men gifted with creative and spiritual genius. The fact that these historical figures have become legends is quite emblematic. But it doesn't matter whether they were incarnate or "collective" personalities, as Guénon put it, because it's their message that counts, the path they have indicated and transmitted over the centuries almost without interruption, sometimes openly, more often secretly, through what has rightly been called a "golden chain."

BB: So we have to mention the names of the men who made this "man's story"?

Major fathers: Hermes, Pythagoras, Moses, Manu, Orpheus

AF: For esotericism, almost just as for Christianity, we could speak of a "major patristics" and a "minor patristics." The great Fathers of esotericism were undoubtedly the mythical Hermes Trismegistus and the historical Pythagoras, comparable to the great "moral law-givers": the biblical Moses and the Hindu Manu. The Egyptian origin of Hermes has now been confirmed by scholars such as Martin Bernal.[1] Pythagoras[2] (6th century BC) is said to have been an ancient Greek philosopher and mathematician who actually lived.

---

[1] 1937–2013. Scholar and historian of British Greece. See his *Black Athena* (Rutgers University Press, 3 vols.).

BB: Are they really the "grandfathers" of all esotericism?

AF: Orpheus must be added, also a mythological character, although the great historian of religions Mircea Eliade believed that he actually existed, prior to Homer.[3] But, to repeat, the historical existence of these characters is of little importance; all that matters is that their names are linked to esoteric orientations and the most archaic primitive initiations.

BB: In what sense can these initiations be called esoteric?

AF: They were esoteric, in the sense that their practices were limited to restricted groups, and access to them was forbidden to ordinary lay people. This extreme confidentiality is one of the characteristics of what we have decided, even today, to define as "esoteric," and it seems to me that, in relation to everything we have said so far, this definition can be accepted and assumed.

BB: There's an obvious practical and ritual aspect to these "ways," but what about the speculative side?

AF: I prefer to avoid the term "speculations" and speak of doctrines or knowledge, so as not to make these contents seem like more or less philosophical digressions or dubious conjectures born of sick or imaginative minds.

---

[2] The name "Pythagoras" is probably a heteronomous name rather than a proper noun. It is composed of two elements, the second of which is certainly ἀγορά (*agora*, "public square") and, according to some sources, the first is Πύθιος (*Pythios*, an epithet of Apollo also designating his oracles, such as the Pythia). In this case, the meaning could be interpreted as "one who exhibits oracles." This is, of course, a supposition.

[3] See the chapter "Orpheus, Pythagoras and the new eschatology" in *A History of Religious Ideas*, vol. 2 (Chicago & London: University of Chicago Press, 1982), 182.

BB: And what were the sources of these doctrines?

AF: I think all this knowledge came from intimate experiences, from "inner revelations" and, in short, from living contact with the "other world." They were, I think, "experiences" that could be compared, so to speak, to those of even contemporary shamans (of which there are still many in the world), induced by particular magical-ritual and ecstatic techniques. I think we'll come back to the merits of these "practices" in subsequent interviews; for now, I'd say this clue will suffice.

BB: Noted! But "mystery religions" or "mystery cults" are also spoken of in this period... What can you say about them?

Mystery religions

AF: This seems to me a perfectly acceptable term. According to linguists, the etymology of the word "mystery" goes back to the Indo-European root *mon*, originally meaning "to close the mouth." From this root come the Greek terms *myō*: "to conceal," *myésis*: "initiation" and *mystés*: "initiated"; hence also "mystical." The common components of mystery rites were usually sacred symbols and magical ceremonies, sacraments and purification rituals, which could include sacrifices, ablutions, fasting or abstinence, devotional banquets, dances, etc.

BB: Some of these mystery religions are still known of today. Can you say a few words about them?

AF: Certainly! There were the "great mysteries" (τὰ μεγάλα μυστήρια) of Eleusis[4] linked to the cult of the rural divini-

---

[4] Twenty kilometers west of Athens.

ties of nature and the seasons, namely Demeter and Perse-phone. Next, I'd highlight cults linked to Dionysus, those linked to the Phrygian deity Sabazios, the mysteries of the Cabiri at Samothrace in the sanctuary of the same name, and, as mentioned above, the Orphic and Pythagorean mysteries. Then come other mystery cults of Eastern origin: those of Asia Minor, of the Great Mother Cybele with Attis, those of Serapis, Isis and Osiris of Egyptian mythol-ogy, and those of Mithra, which originated in Persia but permeated imperial Rome.

BB: These are very widespread realities, popular cults and present in almost all ancient civilizations. But wasn't esoter-icism something elitist?

AF: Actually, only in certain cases; that's why we speak of "mystery religions," precisely to signify their broader, "soc-ial" connotations. In fact, there was also this whole "popu-lar esotericism": an esotericism within everyone's reach, just as today there is an esoteric and initiatory organization like Freemasonry with millions of adherents worldwide.

BB: Returning to the "fathers" of esotericism, you men-tioned "minor fathers." Who would you put in this cate-gory?

Esoteric patristics and scholasticism

AF: A long list could be drawn up: from Plato to René Guénon. But I wanted to introduce this category not so much to talk about the individual figures we can discuss in a future interview, but to draw a semantic parallel between esotericism and the Christian religion. This can help us understand a great deal about esotericism and the historical events associated with it. So, I maintain that the history of esotericism is above all a history of "fathers," both major and minor, and of masters, who defended a perspective, reworked pre-existing materials, formulated solutions, indicated paths, provided practical guidelines, built speculative theoretical architectures, reconciled doctrines and symbols, founded schools and brotherhoods exactly as our "Church fathers" did.

BB: Would you go so far as to speak of esoteric patristics?

AF: I'd say so. And we could also speak of scholastics—for there were many who collected the teachings of these masters and ensured a more or less faithful continuity—and even a scholasticism, for there were just as many who, by dint of formalizing the message, reduced it to something rigid and mechanical, arid and sterile.

BB: It's a very interesting and original way of telling the story of esotericism.

AF: (laughs). Let's just say that I'm trying to simplify the discussion as much as possible, but introducing concepts and categories that can help situate esotericism in a very complex and, as I've already said, rather chaotic context.

BB: What other historical elements would you like to add?

Esotericism: geography of historical origins

AF: I believe that, complementarily, geographical elements need to be introduced. Geography is certainly essential for understanding history, but, particularly here, it's also essential for understanding the evolution or involution of thought.

BB: That's right; so which geographical areas are most involved in the history of esotericism?

AF: I'd call them "centers of irradiation" and propagation. A new discipline, "religious geography," is already dealing with this, but to my knowledge, it has not yet examined the history of esotericism. Let's hope it does so in the future, as there's no shortage of material for in-depth study.

BB: So, what were the main "centers of irradiation" for esotericism?

AF: In the West, it was mainly Egypt (Heliopolis and Saïs) and Hellas (Eleusis, Delphi, Olympia); in the Middle East, Iraq (Najaf) and Iran (Qom); in the East, Tibet (Lhasa). But there were countless other centers, some of which did not survive. They may also have been pilgrimage destinations, or places where inexplicable events had occurred. Today, we tend to dismiss these possibly factual occurrences as legends, myths, and fantasies, and no doubt in some cases they were, but not always, I think. Divine manifestations (theophanies in the language of historians of religion) are by no means human inventions, and even the most skeptical reader should be aware of this.

BB: Let's hope so (laughs). As for Asia, you mentioned Tibet, but in China and Japan there are clearly esoterisms linked to some locations, aren't there?

AF: That's right. For Japan, I'm thinking of Mount Fuji, but also of Osorezan, the volcanic Mountain of Hell that rises in the center of the Shimokita peninsula, in the far north of Aomori prefecture. Walking on its slopes is equivalent to entering the Buddhist lands of the afterlife. For China, I would also mention the sacred mountains, numerous and spread over different areas, where there are often temples where it is possible to receive an initiation. One of these mountains is home to the famous Shaolin monastery, an important temple in the history of Chinese Buddhism, recognized as the cradle of *Chan* Buddhism and the birthplace of *Shaolin quan*.

BB: For my part, I don't know if the cosmogenetic esotericism of the Dogons in Africa is linked to a particular place, such as the famous Bandiagara cliff...

Esotericism and Gnosticism

Getting back to history, would you agree that Gnosticism, Manichaeism, or the Alexandrian school are part of the history of esotericism?

AF: In a way, yes, but Gnosticism is too vast and complex a phenomenon to fit entirely into the category of esotericism. I've spoken of scholastics and scholasticism; here I'd rather speak of heresies and "sectarian" phenomena. In Gnosticism in general, there is not only the choice of a part instead of the whole, but also the shadow of "Polemos."[5]

BB: Polemos the war demon of Greek mythology?

AF: Yes, that's the one! What I'm trying to say here is that, generally speaking, the generic term "Gnosticism" covers doctrines that have, for the most part, proved hostile to institutional traditions, both civil and religious, and that this hostility, distrust, and aversion have little to do with the search for truth, and therefore with esotericism. It is for this reason that I would tend to exclude them from the history of authentic esoteric traditions, even though I am aware that an esoterologist would have much to say.

---

[5] From "*polemos*" comes the Italian word "*polemica*," the French "polémique," and the English "polemic."

BB: So, do you think it will be important to come back to it later?

AF: Absolutely. When we talk about Christian esotericism or Jewish esotericism, we won't be able to avoid it.

Esotericism and philosophical schools

BB: In the context of this overview of the history of esotericism, do you see any other essential pointers? For example, what about Alexandrian gnosis and Neoplatonism?

AF: What I'm saying is that they were, in fact, schools, that is, places of study that catered to certain intellectual dispositions of those who attended them, but they were certainly not initiatory organizations or esoteric currents. Of course, in these schools there were "masters" who taught, and these teachers could also have been initiates, I don't deny it. But I frankly find it hard to describe these schools as esoteric at all. As far as Neoplatonism is concerned, we're dealing with a cultural phenomenon, even if it has many sapiential and therefore, in a way, esoteric implications.

BB: Do we stop here? What about alchemy, the Kabbalah...?

AF: These are two "manifestations" of esotericism, and are certainly part and parcel of the history of esotericism.

BB: Phew, I was afraid you'd left them out! (laughs)

AF: No, no, please! (laughs). There are undoubtedly two currents of esotericism which, not coincidentally, have a historically uncertain origin. According to the historians, the first (alchemy) appeared in the eighth century, while the second (Kabbalah) in the twelfth. But even the most rigorous historians understand that there were certainly antecedents. The explanation of a creation through syncretism is rather weak, but, for want of a better word, it's the one I'm sticking with.

BB: I understand. Shall we end this interview on the history of esotericism? Is there anything else you'd like to add?

AF: No, I would stop here, also because we will necessarily continue to mention historical aspects of esotericism in the remainder of this series of interviews, and corroborative or complementary elements will be added of their own accord.

Chapter 5
Esotericism and Esotericists

Despite the immense variety of esotericisms, is it possible to sketch out a classification, and among the multiplicity of esotericists, is it possible to evoke a few great names? Here are two fundamental questions.

BB: Does the great diversity of esotericism nevertheless allow us to sketch out a classification?

An esoteric classification

AF: Esotericism, the kind I define as authentic—and I've tried to explain why—is fundamentally and essentially a Way. But a way to what? I'd answer: a path to Truth.

BB: A rather different definition from that of academic works, in two ways: firstly, as we've seen, because you reject the inauthentic from esotericism, and secondly, because it's no longer simply a question of developing interpretations or simply knowledge, but in that it's a path, involving the person who follows it.

AF: Absolutely! And it's precisely for this second reason that in this interview I'd like to try and explain myself better, by first clarifying the meaning of the word "truth." *Quid est veritas?* ("What is truth?") is what Pontius Pilate asked Jesus—asked Jesus, but received no answer. Initiatic language is made up of silences, because truth is inexpressible.

BB: But esoteric literature is made up of a lot of words, and a cryptic language that often has to be deciphered. How do you explain this contradiction?

AF: This is because human beings can't do without language in any case, but it's the truth of language that interests the esotericist. The truth of language also means the evocative power of the word, the power of the word itself, the power of the sound that expresses the word, and the power of the silence that follows it.

BB: The search for truth is therefore also a search for the truth *of language!*

AF: Exactly. And here we already have the possibility of a first classification: there's the "mute" esotericism, the one without manuals, so to speak; there's the "oral" esotericism of the masters; and finally, there's the "written" esotericism of the pupils, disciples, and followers. We base the history of esotericism above all on the written word, on books, but then we can't help considering that the best part of these teachings remains unknown to us: it's *de facto* intangible.

Thus, the first and second subdivisions correspond to patristics, and the third to scholastics and scholasticism.

BB: This is most intriguing! (laughs). So let's start with this "patristics." Who are these fathers?

A patristics of esotericism

AF: I've already mentioned them: Orpheus, Pythagoras, and Hermes Trismegistus, three names everyone knows and about which thousands and thousands of pages have been written. They are the true fathers of esotericism. Mythical fathers, as we've said, who were given a symbolic name, which surely—whether or not it's accepted that they were real individuals—was not their "baptismal name." I would also point out that these three names are all of Greek origin. This means that the contribution made by the peoples of these lands to esotericism was fundamental. But then we have to ask ourselves what Hellas really was, and what peoples and cultures converged there. But that's a subject we can't go into here. Just keep it in mind.

BB: You mentioned Pythagoras. Could you also say something about the meaning of the names "Hermes" and "Orpheus"?

AF: Of course. Hermes Trismegistus, as we've said, is certainly a legendary figure from the pre-Classical era, revered as a master of wisdom and traditionally regarded as the author of the *Corpus Hermeticum.* He is credited with founding the esoteric movement known as Hermeticism. Hermes Trismegistus literally means "Hermes the thrice-great." With this name, the Greeks equated him with the *god* Hermes, god of the logos and communication, but also with Thoth the Egyptian god of letters, numbers, and geometry. As it was customary among the Egyptians to repeat the adjective "great" before the name of deities, Hermes was precisely named the thrice-great (*tris-megisto*).

BB: And Orpheus?

AF: The Greek name "*Orpheus*" is actually of unknown origin, but for which various hypotheses have been put forward, including one that links this name to *orphne*, "the darkness of night" or to *orphanós*, "orphan," "alone"; but there is no agreement among linguists.

BB: How would you sum up what the etymologies of the names of these "fathers" of esotericism tell us?

AF: They tell us fundamental things about true esotericism. The name Pythagoras tells us that esotericism conveys oracular knowledge (the link with Apollo, god of music, the medical arts, the sciences, the intellect, and prophecy), but reserved, in the sense that those who really listen and think have always been a tiny minority. What's more, the connection with the *agora*, the public square, tells us precisely the collective nature of this name, which I take to mean that it's the wisdom or truth that counts, not the individuality who transmits it.

BB: Among other things, it seems that the Pythagorean school also welcomed women, who were generally excluded from esoteric teachings. Is this true?

AF: Yes, in part. This *conventio ad excludendum*[1] with regard to women concerned their presumed inability to attempt certain rational and spiritual disciplines. Even today, a traditionally and historically "initiatory" institution such as Freemasonry finds it hard to accept the presence of women in lodges, and that says a lot about the persistence of this idea.[2] This was not at all the case in the Pythagorean school, nor in "mystery religions" and early Christianity, as also in many other fields. We'll have to come back to this theme.

[1] Latin term used to define an explicit agreement or tacit understanding between social parties whose purpose was to exclude a specific third party from certain forms of alliance, participation or collaboration.
[2] The so-called Anderson Constitutions, which for nearly three centuries have been the law within the Masonic institution, in the third chapter state the following: "Persons admitted as members of a Lodge must be good and sincere men, free-born and of mature and wise age, not slaves, not women, not immoral or scandalous men, but of good repute."

BB: Certainly! If we stick to names for now: what does the name "Hermes" tell us about the nature of esotericism?

AF: Hermes is the mediator god between men and the gods, analogous to the Latin Mercury and the Egyptian Thoth. The word comes from the Greek *Ermes/Eiro,* meaning "announcement." He takes his name from the son of Zeus and Maia, the god of theft and commerce, messenger of the gods and psychopomp, "companion of souls." Hermeticism comes from his name, and "hermeticism" is synonymous with "esotericism." The most appropriate dimension of esotericism, then, is that of something between heaven and earth, between microcosm and macrocosm, or between cosmos and metacosm. Esotericism brings mankind "the fire of the gods," not by "stealing" it, as in the case of Prometheus, but as a "gift."

BB: Following your reasoning, we could say that false esotericism is Promethean, whereas true esotericism is not.

AF: Absolutely. It's a parameter of discernment. It brings us back to the parallel with "grace," which we discussed in a previous interview.

BB: Does the name Hermes tell us even more?

AF: It also tells us that esotericism has an enigmatic, closed, and sometimes even incomprehensible dimension (this is the meaning we usually attribute to the word "hermetic"). A secret that is such, not because it is abstruse, but because no reasoning can grasp it, no thought, however profound, can violate it—only the Spirit holds the keys. This is what Jesus said: "Blessed are you, Simon, son of Jonah, for flesh and blood has not revealed this to you, but—

my Father who is in heaven."[3] Hermes is also a figure of the *Logos*, but the *Logos* of the gods, with a capital "L." When the Logos of the gods becomes word, teaching, it also becomes literature, but it is the literature of the gods. Esotericism as a "literary genre" is thus "the literature of the gods."

BB: Very interesting! And Orpheus?

AF: We said that Orpheus is generally translated as "obscure," "alone." This is because Orpheus, like Pythagoras, has to do with Apollo and with the magic of song, sound, and voice—elements that play an important part in esotericism. What's more, Orpheus is the one who "descends into the underworld." And indeed, the esotericist is not only a loner (someone who doesn't like to socialize too much, who leads a secluded life and appears in public as little as possible), but when he does appear, he always tries to conceal his status and interests—which corresponds to a certain familiarity with death, with the dead and with the afterlife.

Dante, the esotericist par excellence

BB: It occurs to me that a hidden presence, derived from the classic myth of Orpheus, is present in Dante's account of his "journey into the other world."

AF: Exactly! And, from this point of view, Dante Alighieri is, in my opinion, the esotericist *par excellence.*

BB: Even though some literary critics and Dante specialists deny Dante's esotericism?

[3] Matt. 16:17.

AF: Yes, they deny it and reduce Dante's speech to a literary fact. But these gentlemen don't understand esotericism, and often, I must say, not even theology or philosophy. If you don't "adhere" to something (adhere, i.e., join something by matching it; being attached to it or in close contact with it), you can't really understand it. In Dante flows the whole pre-Christian classical tradition (in the *Divine Comedy*, there's much Pythagoreanism and also Hermeticism), transmitted into the Christian theological and philosophical tradition. It's not a simple form of irenicism or ecumenism, as we'd say today, but a true synthesis, a true esotericism, a *summa summarum* as I've already said.

BB: Dante a "father" of esotericism, or a pupil?

AF: Dante is a schoolboy, but a very, very good one! (laughs). And after all, so was Plato, since his teacher was Socrates. You could probably call him a "father."

Socrates esotericist

BB: Socrates an esotericist!

AF: You bet! An esotericist of the "loner" type, without a school. All his knowledge and wisdom, according to his best pupil, Plato, came from an "inner voice," the famous *daimon*.

BB: What does his "esotericism" consist of?

AF: When knowledge is not derived from a human source, we can define it as esoteric. On the other hand, at Delphi, in the famous sanctuary we've already mentioned, Socrates was considered the wisest man in Greece. So it was the initiates themselves who designated him as a "master," or rather a spokesman for the gods.

BB: Are there any other fathers you'd like to mention?

AF: No, I'd stop at Socrates. And in his case, as perhaps in the case of Pythagoras, we're talking about real people, not myths.

BB: At this point, we should try to say something about "esoteric scholasticism." You mentioned Plato and Dante. Would you eliminate Aristotle?

AF: Not at all. And how could I exclude "the master of those who know" (Dante)?[4]

Aristotle esotericist

BB: Aristotle that great unknown!

AF: Exactly! There's a big misunderstanding about Aristotle. The conventional image of Aristotle is of a sort of pure scholar and logical, rigorous philosopher, forgetting or bracketing his metaphysical, spiritual, and contemplative orientation, and, perhaps, his ties to the mystery traditions.[5]

BB: Without a doubt. Among other things, it's from his lexicon that, in a certain sense, the word "esotericism" is drawn.

AF: That's right! Aristotle very often used the word "exotericism," and even if the adjective "esoteric" was created later, it could not have been conceived without the term that precedes it. Secondly, there's a whole debate about what Aristotle really meant by the word "exoteric." Some scholars believe, with good arguments, that the Philosopher

---

[4] *Divine Comedy,* Inferno, IV, 131.

[5] On this subject rests the meticulous study of the professor of ancient and patristic philosophy, Abraham P. Bos (1943): *Cosmic and Meta-Cosmic Theology in Aristotle's Lost Dialogues* (Leiden: Brill, 1989).

was referring to those realities which are "outside" (*exo*) and thus beyond physical nature. It is these realities that were later described as "esoteric" and "meta-physical."[6]

BB: So almost a reversal of meaning!

AF: That's right. In other words, if we miss the meaning of certain words used by the ancients, we also run the risk of completely missing what they said.

BB: So we have to go back to "the truth of language," as you said...

AF: This would be necessary, assuming the rest of us manage to understand it, because what can't be recovered is the mentality of the ancients, so different and so far removed from our own. Here, too, lie the difficulties of reconstructing not only history, but also the notion of esotericism.

BB: You're right! Let's go back to the esoteric Aristotle. A scholastic esotericist, if I understand correctly.

AF: Absolutely! Scholastic speech and writing. He gave esotericism an extraordinary impetus, both formal and substantial, both direct and indirect. He gave it with his public and private teachings, through his Peripatetic school (from the Greek *Peripatos*: path, walk), where his pupils gathered, and which was not by chance a sanctuary dedicated to Apollo Licio—hence the school's other name: the Lyceum. But he also gave this impulse through his spirit, whose presence is still felt after two thousand six hundred years. How many stimuli came from him, at every level! Then

---

[6] Ibid. One should be mindful as well of the term "acroamatic" widely used by Aristotle and others of his contemporaries, signifying "reserved to those near at hand and to close associates."

there are the lost works. The so-called "scientific works," it must be understood, were never more than a propaedeutic.

BB: Esoterologist Pierre A. Riffard, whom you mentioned in a previous interview and recommended for further reading, believes that Aristotle was only a "technician of philosophy" and not a specialist in the occult.

AF: And I partly agree. But Aristotle was surely initiated into the mysteries and a guardian of Tradition, like his master Plato. That certainly can't be denied. Nor can it be denied that almost everyone draws inspiration from him, precisely because his thought was a *summa summarum*, an esotericism, a total vision of reality and about reality.

BB: Esotericism as a "total vision of reality"…

AF: Esotericism is just that: total knowledge and a total point of view that leaves nothing out, not even science, not even logic. It's a system in which "everything fits together."

BB: But if esotericism is a "way," a path to truth, how is it compatible with a "system"?

AF: The word was probably ill-chosen, but let's just say that this "path" leaves no stone unturned. It's a path that engages the whole man, and therefore also his thinking, his ideas, his vision of the world. What is guessed can be explained, and what is explained can be guessed again, known, precisely through its enunciation and explanation. Esotericism is like a cathedral, a perfect construction with many structural, architectural, or functional elements, as well as decorative ones. Focusing on the details can make you lose sight of the whole, but it's the whole that takes precedence, along with the foundations on which it rests.

BB: It's a fascinating analogy, but let's get back to the "scholastic esotericists," lest we lose the logical thread of an Aristotelian-style discourse (laughs).

Scholastic schools and esotericists

AF: Of course, you're right. However, all these steps, backwards or sideways, are precisely what's needed to push us ever further, forcing us to rethink what we've always thought we knew and understood about esotericism.

Let's get back to the names. I don't want to give too many of them, because the list would be interminable, not to mention the few words we'd need to say about each one. Instead, let's talk about currents, while remaining within the sphere of scholasticism and "esoteric schoolchildren" (more names can be cited in an interview devoted to occultism and "modern" esotericism). So, in this scholastic category, I would include the whole of the vast Neo-Platonic movement.

BB: There are a lot of names. Can you recall the most important ones?

AF: I'd like to mention the schools first:

— the school of Rome, founded by Plotinus and continued by his disciples Porphyrius and Amelius;

— the Alexandrian school, founded by Ammonios Saccas which included Olympiodorus the Elder, the philosopher Hypatia and her father Theon;

— the Syriac school of Apamea, founded by Iamblichus, a disciple of Porphyry which distinguished itself by its revision of the founder's theories, and by its marked revival of Neo-Pythagorean traditions and the wisdom contained in the so-called *Corpus Hermeticum*;

— the school of Athens, linked to the Syriac school by Priscus, whose major representatives were Plutarch of Athens and Syrianus, and the fruits of which are attested to in the works of Proclus;

— the Pergamon school, founded by Edesios of Cappadocia, which had one of its principal representatives in the person of the emperor Julian;

— the Alexandrian theological school or Didascalea, which attributed its foundation directly to St Mark the Evangelist, first with Panthenus ("the Sicilian bee"), then Clement of Alexandria.

BB: Christian Neoplatonism...

AF: In full, first of all with St. Denys the Areopagite[7] and John Scotus Eriugena, followed by Hildegarde of Bingen, Master Eckhart, Margaret Ebner, Henry Suso, John Tauler, Rulman Merswin, Nicholas of Cusa, Marsilio Ficino, Pico della Mirandola, and Giordano Bruno, as well as the medieval mystical group, the "Friends of God" (14th c.).

BB: And after the Renaissance?

AF: The chain continues with other figures such as Schelling, Schopenhauer, the Cambridge Platonists Ralph Cudworth and Henry More, the American transcendentalists,

---

[7] Known for a time as "Pseudo-Denys the Areopagite" not to be confused with the bishop of Athens (1st century), or even St. Denis of Paris. Today, it is generally accepted that this is a tradition that dates back to the first century and was crystallized around the year 500, so we can do away with the inelegant "pseudo."

especially Emerson and Thoreau, down to the "traditional thinkers" of the 20th century, a movement inaugurated by René Guénon, followed by Julius Evola, Ananda K. Coomaraswamy, Titus Burckhardt, Frithjof Schuon, Elémire Zolla, Henry Corbin, Alain Daniélou, Martin Lings, Seyyed Hossein Nasr, and many others. In some respects, the psychoanalyst Carl Gustav Jung can also be included in the esotericism of the 20th century, even if, for some, he was nothing more than a "gnostic," and in the worst sense of the word.

Guénon esotericist

BB: Aren't you giving too much weight to the "Traditionalist Thinkers"?

AF: Yes, I recognize my addiction to this "current" which I hold in the highest esteem.

BB: Do you find them truly in harmony with the esotericism of the "founding fathers"?

AF: I think so, so much so that with their works we could even speak of a neo-patristics of esotericism. But beware: the "father" is René Guénon—all the others are more or less good pupils.

BB: Then Guénon would be on the level of a Pythagoras?

AF: I would be tempted to say so. But then you'd have to consider that there's a "father of esotericism" Guénon and a "pupil of esotericism" Guénon. As Goethe would have said, alas, "two souls lived in his breast": that of the scholar who writes and speaks, and that of the "mute" initiate. I believe his posterity has understood the first aspect above all, while only a few have detected and benefited from the second.

The Guénon scholastics either faithfully repeated the master's letter, or at least tried to do so, whereas the Guénonist schoolchildren froze it uncritically in hollow formulas—a fine example, indeed, of scholasticism! I think the Guénon *insider* has been little understood. And this "initiate" certainly wouldn't have wanted his name placed before the sacred doctrine. Paraphrasing St John the Evangelist, whose name (Yahya) Guénon certainly didn't adopt as his "name in religion" by chance: "He must increase and I must decrease" (John 3:30)—i.e., my message and my person have been placed at the service of God, at the service of the One; and no, they will never take His place! Those who idolized Guénon by betraying his true message should remember this.

BB: Can we say then that "fathers" (with a lower-case f), to be such, must defer to the "Father" (with an upper-case F)?

AF: Yes, you could say that. And let's add that there's no real esotericism outside this hierarchical subordination.

BB: From this point of view, although we can come back to it, Aristotle nevertheless *broke* with Plato, his teacher of quasi twenty years (from 367 to 347 BC, death of Plato). For the latter, the world has an iconic function, and knowledge of it, can only be hypothetical—"a plausible myth," he says (*Timaeus*, 29d)—because the visible image refers to an invisible Model (cf. *Timaeus*, 29b). From this stems all possible symbolic knowledge.

Aristotle, on the other hand, adopts the perspective of a philosophy of nature, of a physics, which he founds, moreover, but where everything is given and only remains to be interpreted.

AF: But Aristotle does have a supernaturalism of intelligible forms, namely his "intelligence comes through the door"[8] and the agent intellect is "immortal and eternal" (*On the Soul,* III, 5).

BB: Yes, but not the world as such. The Philosopher denies the intelligible world, which is reduced to the visible world, thanks to which he is able to found science: it is the radical ontological distinction between the object to be known and the knowing subject that guarantees the objectivity of science. In doing so, he remains with the hypothetico-deductive knowledge brought about by discursive reason (*dianoia*); we remain in the world of concepts, on the plane of the conceivable and in the domain of the learned, compared to the intuitive knowledge of the intellect (*noesis*) which, according to Plato, then opens up the world of Ideas or meaning on the plane of the intelligible to a possible true metaphysical knowledge.

---

[8] *On the Generation of Animals,* II 3, 736 a, 27 b 12.

Chapter 6

An Esoteric Adventure

With two works both titled, Lighted by Books, *and* Following the Reading Quest of a "Knight-Errant," *one published in 2007 and the other in 2022,[1] Aldo La Fata presents, albeit indirectly through reviews of works written by others, a journey, an adventure, one might say, into esotericism.*

BB: Could you illustrate your esoteric "adventure," this time not in the light of personal events (cf. chap. 2, Esoteric biography), but through successive encounters with key people and books.

Panunzio, a Christian metaphysics

ALS. Certainly. I mentioned the books by Evola and Guénon and the momentous encounter for me with the work of Silvano Panunzio, in particular his *Contemplazione e Simbolo. Summa iniziatica orientale-occidentale* [Contemplation and Symbol. An East-West initiatory summa] (Roma: Ed. Volpe, 1976).

BB: What was so special about it?

AF: The author heralded the existence of a Christian metaphysics, initiation, and esotericism. I had strongly doubted that Christianity possessed these elements.

BB: And did reading this book convince you?

---

[1] *Nella luce dei libri. Parcorsi di lettura di un "cavaliere errante,"* Boopen Editore, 2007 and, under the same title, Solfanelli, 2022.

AF: Straight away! In this book, Panunzio has succeeded in demonstrating that Christianity was much more than "the religion that imposed itself on the West," as Evola liked to say…

BB: This reminds me of my uncle, a priest at the Oratory and a great joker, who used to joke, in the manner of Evola, that a religion is a successful sect…

AF: I can see the irony! But Christianity is infinitely more, with, as Panunzio says, chests full of treasures. You just have to open them to be amazed.

BB: Of course, all you have to do is open the books by Panunzio. Plus, to convince readers, if they weren't so already, you've orchestrated practically all the reissues, including two in France recently. Have you met other authors like Panunzio along the way?

Paolo Virio, a Christian esotericist

AF: Yes, there was Paolo Marchetti, known as Paolo Virio (1910–1969). I found his books in the famous Roman esoteric bookshop "Rotondi"[2] in the Via Merulana, near the two great basilicas of Saint John Lateran and Santa Maria Maggiore. Reading *Paolo M. Virio: Esempio di vita*,[3] written by his wife Luciana after his death, was decisive. The life of this unknown Christian esotericist was told as if in a captivating novel. There were his ideas, his readings, his studies, his encounters with other contemporary esotericists, clues

---

[2] Amedeo Rotondi, also known by the pseudonyms Amadeus Voldben and Vico di Varo (1908–1999), an esotericist, founded it in the late 1930s, and after almost a century, incredibly, it's still here.

[3] Rome: Edizioni Sophia, 1971. Reissued in 2003 by Simmetria.

to the "binomial" path of initiation,[4] followed with conviction alongside his wife. In short, through this text, esotericism has left books behind and entered into real life.

BB: And even today, it seems, you still have the same respect for this author.

AF: Yes, I can confirm that. You should know that after reading this book I decided to meet the author, Mrs Luciana Virio, born Adelina Sgabelloni (1904–2000), quickly becoming her confidant and friend.

BB: Have you joined this "binomial school"?

AF: No, because in reality there was no school or organization behind their experiment.[5] What's more, I was single at the time and would have had to be married to a woman with the same convictions and initiatory intentions.

BB: I'd love to ask you about your friendship with Mrs Virio, but we'd probably be straying from the subject. So let's get on with meeting people or books.

AF: I should mention a second book, also edited by Luciana, which was just as important to me as the first: the *Corrispondenza iniziatica* [Initiatic Correspondence] (Roma: Centarini, 1970). It's no coincidence that this text was published in an enlarged edition, after 2000, in a single volume with the biography we've been talking about. Virio's correspondents were mostly friends who were very interested in his testimony and who considered him a master or, *at the very least,* an authentic and serious representative of Chris-

---

[4] From an alchemical point of view, we could say it's a "two-vessel path," traditionally a form of Christian tantrism.

[5] The Virios Christian esotericism, according to a reconstruction carried out by the couple, goes back as far as the First Crusade, i.e., around the year 1000, but unfortunately there are no documents to prove this.

tian esotericism. Among these correspondents was René Guénon's well-known Italian collaborator Corrado Rocco.[6]

BB: And what were the subjects of these letters?

AF: They spoke of esoteric authors, books, and doctrines... I remember in particular a valuable explanation of "reincarnation" or metempsychosis, far removed from the banalities and theosophical simplifications I had read up to that point; also, enlightening judgments on outstanding figures of esotericism of the 19th and 20th centuries: Evola (known and met personally), Kremmerz, Papus, Guénon, Schuon, and other famous authors in this vein.

BB: I confess I had never heard of Virio, but, from what you say, he seems a worthy character.

AF: Certainly. Of course, these days, his figure is very much faded, and his books (all published posthumously), apart from those I've mentioned and which, for me, were decisive on many esoteric issues, I could never suggest as essential reading.

BB: Are there any other important books to mention?

The science of magicians

AF: For esotericism in the strict sense, I'd say that two really vital texts are *La Scienza dei Magi* [The Science of the Magi] (Roma: Mediterranee, 1974) by Giuliano Kremmerz, and *Introduzione alla magia* [Introduction to Magic] (Roma: Mediterranee, 1974) by the Ur Group. An entire book would not suffice to comment on these two works alone.

---

[6] Famous esoteric scholar, promoter of the Edizioni Studi Initiati in Naples, in contact with the Blois metaphysician, some of whose most important books he edited and translated into Italian.

BB: Can you still say a few words about them?

AF: I can give it a try. I'll start with Kremmerz. Who was he? Born Ciro Formisano,[7] he is undoubtedly the most important Italian esotericist and hermeticist of the last two centuries, the latest link in a chain that has continued down the centuries to the present day: from Giambattista della Porta (c. 1535–1615) to Giordano Bruno (1548–1600), from Raimondo di Sangro (1710–1771) to Cagliostro (1743–1795), from Pasquale De Servis (1868–1893) to Giustiniano Lebano (1893–1910). And after Kremmerz a chain continued with Rocco Armentano (1886–1966) and Arturo Reghini (1878–1946), as well as Giacomo Boni (1859–1925) and Roggero Musmeci Ferrari Bravo (1868–1937).

BB: And then the "chain" was broken?

AF: (laughs) Hard to say, but I suppose not. And actually, there are other names that could be mentioned, those of living people; so, in order not to offend anyone, I prefer not to mention them.

BB: I understand. So let's get back to that book you called so important: "The Science of the Magi"; what does it contain?

AF: The subtitle gives an idea: "Initiation to the science of magicians; elements of natural and divine magic." The book contains a profusion of Hermetic doctrines, elements of classical magic, descriptions of "occult phenomena and powers," subtle and invisible worlds, and so on. In short, a little of everything we moderns usually imagine to be associated with esotericism, more or less. In any case, I have to admit that reading this potpourri clarified for me a lot

[7] Portici, April 8, 1861–Beausoleil, May 7, 1930.

about esotericism. Above all, I understood the ballast elements with which an esotericist can weigh himself down and then jettison.

BB: What are these items to be jettisoned?

AF: The more properly magical aspects in a lower, psychic sense; the famous "powers" that one can undoubtedly acquire with certain practices (and I'm not kidding when I say they're real); familiarity with impersonal forces that can take over and undermine the personality, perhaps ending up feeding instinctive and irrational impulses that are then difficult to govern.

BB: How worrying!

AF: Yes, and it really is! Some have ended up in an asylum, or even worse.

BB: If this is esotericism, God forbid!

AF: In reality, it's anti-esotericism or what I've called false esotericism.

BB: Or what has been termed occultism, to distinguish it. One, esotericism, is turned inwards and upwards, the other, with powers to be developed and put to work, is turned outwards and downwards.

AF: Absolutely. The problem is that, in the universe, every force, every current, meets its opposite; and then again, every Way can become complicated into a labyrinth in which we end up getting lost or plunging into a bottomless pit. But I'm afraid this applies to everything, even the most sacred and spiritual religions like Buddhism and Christianity. How many inappropriate behaviors can result from a misunderstanding of a Way!

BB: Indeed, whether we think of fanaticism or the exploitation of the weakest!

Introduction to magic

AF: Another fundamental text in my esoteric studies was that collective work already mentioned, *Introduction to Magic*, by the Ur Group.

BB: Magic again! (laughs)

AF: (laughs) Well, yes and no, because in this case we're dealing with more heterogeneous material. It's about magic, it's true, but there's much more to it than that. In fact, I'd go so far as to say that it's the most important work on esotericism of the 20th century, as so many of its possible forms, including religious and metaphysical, are represented. In my opinion, there's nothing else like it in the world. In these books (the Italian edition came out in three volumes, as did the Kremmerz), there is the combined effort of the best esotericists of the last century.

BB: From the way you talk about it, it sounds like this book has fascinated you.

AF: Yes, partly. Once you've read this book, you feel you know everything about esotericism, or at least everything you need to know.

BB: So who were the "esotericists" behind this editorial adventure?

AF: It was a partnership, a sort of heterogeneous initiatory circle, which had taken the name of *Gruppo di Ur* [Ur Group]. The phonetic expression "our" in Chaldean and Runic means fire, bull, or ram. As we know, Ur was also the name of one of the most remote settlements in lower Mesopotamia, as well as a Germanic prefix referring to something primitive. This group, made up of exceptional personalities, had its own journal, whose title was precisely "ur" (later changed to "krur"), and it is the articles from this journal that were merged into the three volumes of the *Introduction...*

BB: Can you list the names of those who wrote in it?

AF: The list is long, and also includes such eccentric Catholics as Guido De Giorgio, Nicola Moscardelli, and Girolamo Comi; illustrious anthroposophists such as Giovanni Colazza (one of Rudolf Steiner's "direct" disciples), Aniceto Del Massa, Arturo Onofri (the poet), and Massimo Scaligero (the older brother of Paolo Virio's wife Luciana); Freemasons and neo-Pythagoreans such as Arturo Reghini and Giulio Parisi; pagan Hermetists such as Corallo Reginelli, and Kremmerzians like Ercole Quadrelli. Even the famous Italian psychoanalyst—the founding father of Italian psychoanalysis—Emilio Servadio was a contributor. And then, of course, there was the group's most important leader, along with Reghini, the famous Julius Evola.

BB: A fine "line-up" of authors, no doubt! (laughs).

AF: Undoubtedly (laughs). It's worth noting that, still young but already very active in the cultural field, Giovanni Battista Montini, the future Pope Paul VI, became interested in this "bevy" and issued an extremely negative judgment.[8] Unfortunately, this judgment reveals the unfamiliarity of the Church of Rome and its "doctors" with certain borderline themes.

[8] The review was published in no. 6 of the Catholic journal *Studium* (1928, 323–24) under the title *Una nuova rivista* [A New Journal].

BB: I'm sure we'll talk about Christian esotericism later. Another milestone in your esoteric reading journey?

Gustav Meyrink

AF: I'd say the novels by Gustav Meyrink[9]: *The Golem* (*Der Golem*, 1915), *The Green Face* (*Das grüne Gesicht*, 1916), *Walpurgis Night* (*Walpurgisnacht. Phantastischer Roman*, 1917), *The White Dominican* (*Der weiße Dominikaner. Aus dem Tagebuch eines Unsichtbaren*, 1921). *The Angel at the Western Window* (*Der Engel vom westlichen Fenster*, 1927). So much could be said about these books and their author, but I'll limit myself here to saying that this Viennese writer, better than many other authors, writers, and essayists who had hitherto dealt with esotericism, had understood, and I would say guessed, the most essential truths, managing to convey them exactly and almost without altering them. In him, there is the surpassing of all the whims and fancies of nineteenth-century occultism. In short, Meyrink was for me a good antidote to the blandishments of false esotericism. At least, that's how I see it.

BB: Guénon, however, would not agree. I remember that he didn't think much of this writer.

AF: Yes, I'm aware of that. I remember reading it in his correspondence with Evola. Evola was known to be a great admirer of Meyrink and almost all the translations of his books into Italian are by him.[10]

BB: But why did Guénon have such a bad impression of him?

---

[9] Gustav Meyrink, pseudonym of Gustav Meyer (Vienna, January 19, 1868–Starnberg, December 4, 1932).

[10] Of course, other translations are also available today.

AF: When Guénon read Meyrink—or at least tried to, as I don't think he read a single book in its entirety—he had already gone far beyond certain subjects and no longer felt the need to return to them. He lived in more limpid and crystalline spiritual atmospheres, and there's no denying that Meyrink's books contain quite a few disturbing elements. Moreover, I would add that Guénon was never interested in fantasy and fiction in general. He was intellectually too "geometric" to indulge, even recreationally, in literary musings.

BB: Yes, that seems quite likely. Speaking of "initiatory" novels, have you read Castaneda's?

AF: Yes, three or four texts, if I remember correctly, but I confess I never found the slightest interest in this much-vaunted author. I don't consider him a milestone in my studies. I know he's very popular with esotericists today, but, personally, I've never liked him. I think I smelled a fraud right from the start. Of course, that's just my opinion, and mine alone.

BB: As it happens, my few glimpses of his texts have never encouraged me to read him either.

AF: Apart from Castaneda and the editorial operation behind it, I confess I've always considered shamanism to be a sub-category of esotericism, a wild and primitive form of esotericism. Obviously, I don't want to generalize, and my judgment naturally refers to certain forms of shamanism and not to shamanism as such, within which I do of course also recognize a "noble lineage," as in the case of Siberian or Amerindian shamanism. For all that, I'm more Apollonian than Dionysian in spirit, and I've always preferred Bach's music to the tom-tom, that is, to the overly caricatured tom-tom.

BB: I share those tastes! Are there any other authors or books you'd like to mention in this brief review of your reading career?

Goethe, Shakespeare, Dante

AF: Oh my God, there would be so many. Perhaps the ones that had the biggest impact on my training were Goethe and Shakespeare. I consider them truly great masters of esotericism and would place them next to Dante Alighieri. I don't think anyone who wants to have the deepest idea of esotericism can ignore them. With them, we're on a par with Homer and Virgil, two other important "signposts" on the path to initiation for those who can understand them.

In their case, we speak of "vati"[11] and, for their works of absolute literature or, as my friend Alain Santacreu would say, "counter-literature." In my opinion, the lessons to be learned from their work far exceed any of the pseudo-esoteric junk produced over the last two hundred years. And I would argue that anyone who reads these authors will sooner or later consign almost all the esoteric junk literature produced over the last two centuries to the dustbin. No Papus, no Aleister Crowley, will ever be able to measure up to these giants.

BB: Are they also good scholastics?

AF: The best of all time, in my opinion. Scholastics who

---

[11] Latin *vatis* (Greek, *ouateis*) is a word of Gaulish origin which designates a seer, a prophet, an oracle.

had the gift of true intelligence and inspiration, as well as exceptional talents for visionary writing.

BB: We're moving quickly towards the conclusion of this interview. Do you have any other "bedside books" you'd like to talk about?

Mircea Eliade

AF: I'd like to end with the novels of Mircea Eliade (1907–1986). After Meyrink, these are the ones to which I owe the most in terms of my understanding of esotericism. These days, they're hardly talked about, and Eliade's star, which shone for several decades in the very firmament of "esotericists," now seems extinguished. Yet the books of this incredible and prolific scholar were an important step in my understanding of myth and religion. It was precisely in his novels that Eliade gave the best of himself. I read them avidly and they contain many keys to understanding esotericism, with sometimes unexpected and surprising painterly touches. These are books I would still recommend to anyone who wants to get an unbiased and unmistakable idea of esotericism, starting with the novels *The Nineteen Roses* and *The Secret of Doctor Honigberger* and continuing with *Wedding in Paradise, The Old Man and the Officer, Forbidden Forest, The Serpent,* and *Youth without Youth.*[12] Here's another effective antidote to the pitfalls of false esotericism.

[12] This 1976 novel, *Tinerete fara de tinerete* (*Youth without Youth,* trans. 1988) was adapted for the cinema by Francis Ford Coppola.

Chapter 7
Esotericism and Mysticism

Is esotericism necessarily mystical in nature? Is a mystical attribute a criterion for differentiating between different esotericisms, or even for establishing a hierarchy? These are questions that needed to be asked.

BB: Do not the mysteries, such as esoteric approaches, necessarily have to be mystical in nature?

Mystical...

AF: It all depends on the meaning given to the word "mystical." The Italian *mistico* (but also its French equivalent *mystique*) derives from the Latin *mysticus*, in turn derived from the ancient Greek *mystikos*, used to designate the mysteries proper to initiatory cults, given that *mystes* meant precisely "initiated." From the 17th century onwards, the word began to be linked to experiences and facts attributable almost exclusively to the sphere of religion and faith.

BB: In fact, the comparative study of religions has given new breadth to the term "mysticism," so that today we speak of "Indian mysticism," "Islamic mysticism," "Buddhist mysticism," and so on.

AF: That's true, even if there's a risk of levelling out different religious experiences, as if they were identical. So let's say that, in common parlance, when we speak of mystics or mysticism, no one thinks of the initiate, but rather thinks of of the religious halo of holiness and its ecstasies.

74

...or mysticism?

BB: It's useful to distinguish the mystical from mysticism. Mysticism is a recent word and concept. It only appeared in French in 1804, under the pen of Benjamin Constant, and is a good example of the scientific approach of grouping together under a single term everything that can, more or less, be related to it, with a high risk of heterogeneity and confusion.

AF: It's this levelling out that I was talking about. Hence the various classifications that have been proposed by different specialists in religious traditions. For example, a historian of Indian philosophy such as Surendranath Dasgupta, who taught Sanskrit and yoga to Mircea Eliade, spoke of sacrificial (or Vedic) mysticism, *Upanisad* mysticism, yoga mysticism, devotional mysticism (*bhakti*) and popular devotional mysticism, as well as mysticism of the Absolute, in reference to the different ways and means of attaining spiritual realization. Everything depends on establishing what the object of mystical experience is, so to speak.

BB: Indeed, these classifications ultimately boil down to a conceptualization of something that remains mysterious and ineffable. Mystical phenomena and the very experience of the divine infinite cannot be reduced to study material.

AF: Moreover, what is experienced in Christian mysticism is not necessarily identical to what is experienced in non-Christian traditions. We're always talking about something beyond the discursiveness of thought, but certainly I don't know how much our Christic mysticism, or what we call Trinitarian mysticism, really has to do with Hindu "liberation" or Buddhist "Awakening."

Spontaneous mysticism

BB: Still in the context of comparative religious studies, we have also spoken of "spontaneous mysticism," i.e., mysticism not preceded by initiation (through a master or a religious school) or obtained through a specific method of meditation or after learning a particular doctrine. In other words, a mysticism that can also be achieved by "lightning" or a kind of "election."

AF: Certainly, but in the vast field of mysticism and the many forms it can take, perhaps we should return to the word "mystery," which can clarify the possible link between esotericism and mysticism.

Mystery, esotericism, and religion

In Catholic theology, mystery is that truth which reason cannot reach, understand, or demonstrate, and which is essentially a matter of faith. These are the mysteries of faith, such as the sanctifying action of the sacraments, the Marian mysteries, and so on. But the relationship between esotericism and mystery seems much closer in some respects. The word esotericism is almost synonymous with the word mystery, whereas it is not with the word religion. In this sense, we could go so far as to say that esotericism is to mystery what religion is to the mystical, and that mystery is to initiation what the mystical is to religion.

BB: Unless you confuse mystery with secrecy...

AF: ...or mysticism with psychic, or even psychotic, experience.

BB: Mystery, as François Chenique has recalled, is by no means the incomprehensible, only the inexpressible, the unspeakable, the ineffable.

AF: Yes, we have to try and restore the truth to words, and to do that, we have to take them on an upward journey. To stop at common meanings would be to miss the best of these words.

BB: And isn't this an esoteric route?

AF: Of course! And it is well to reflect on this; the greatest speculative minds of all time, both East and West, from Plato to Cusanus, from Sankara to Nagarjuna, have always used a precise, detailed, and always lofty vocabulary. St Thomas Aquinas in his Summa Theologica taught us to interpret all the words of the Gospels by bringing them back to their truest, most authentic meaning. The great Dominican understood that the terms of Sacred Scripture—including periods and commas!—are of decisive importance for understanding the faith.

BB: Among the philosophers of the 20th century, Heidegger is perhaps the one who gave most weight to etymologies. I'm thinking, for example, of his very accurate treatment of the Greek term *alétheia*, which he translates as "elimination of obscurity," or "unveiling." This privative alpha takes away the truth of mystery—*lanthano*, "I am invisible, I am hidden"[1]—and makes it almost its exact opposite.

AF: That's the idea: truth as evidence and mystery as concealment. In fact, the Greek *mystérion* is related to the verb *myein*: "to close, to lock," and refers to mythos: mute. Mystery remains a mystery until it is fathomed. When it is fathomed, it becomes truth. It is this unveiling that we have defined as "mystical experience," although the word "expe-

---

[1] Rendered in German with "*verborgen sein*," to be hidden, concealed.

rience" does not convey the idea of what comes from within (*ab intra*), but rather from without (*ad extra*).

BB: Would you say, then, that esotericism keeps the mystery where religion shows it? I'm thinking of the immense work of the Church Fathers and theologians.

AF: Esotericism and religion both try to preserve mystery, but in different ways. Theology makes abundant use of the word "mystery": "mystery of faith," "sacramental mystery," "mystery of the Holy Trinity," "mystery of salvation," etc. Esotericism is more familiar with "secrecy," i.e., content or experiences that we don't want to reveal, and rightly so, in order to avoid misunderstandings and confusion of planes; in essence, it's the gospel saying: "Do not cast pearls before swine." (Matt. 7:6)

Sometimes esoteric doctrines, those we obviously know from the books that talk about them, explain much more than religion explains to believers. Religion, historically at any rate, seems to leave the believer at the threshold of mystery, even blocking the way and not letting him in; esotericism, for its part, does indeed block the way for the profane, but opens the doors wide for the initiated.

BB: And what about mysticism?

AF: Mysticism, at least for Christianity, is indeed a crossing of the threshold, but, let's say, without having had its approval. This is why mystics are almost always regarded by religious orthodoxy with vigilant suspicion. Acquired or "revealed" truths are, more often than not, "personal" and therefore untransmissible.

BB: Can we say that the mystic enters the mystery, almost unwittingly, by a special grace acting within him? Should we really grant Guénon the passivity of the mystical states he denounces?

AF: In fact, rather not. Assuming there is such a thing as "passivity," we're not talking about inertia, but a clear awareness of one's own nothingness, a trusting surrender, a pious submission, a wise renunciation, a sublime submission... Let's call it humility or "non-acting action," to use a Chinese Taoist expression.

BB: Back to the link between esotericism and mysticism!

Esotericism and mysticism

AF: To begin with, I would say that the two terms belong to semantic areas that are not exactly opposed, but are quite different.

BB: Certainly, but don't they always refer to the same experience: that of something, of a quality, that lies beyond ourselves, "beyond the veil of maya" as the Hindus would say? To say that the esoteric approach has a mystical character, in my opinion, gives esotericism its dignity and brings it back within the realm of the authentically sacred, or, as Guénon would say: "in the wake of the sacred," "in the wake of Tradition."

AF: Yes, I can certainly agree with that. After all, we could also speak of mystical esotericism and esoteric mysticism to mark the distance from magical esotericism and false esotericism.

BB: And where would you see the point of convergence between a mystic and an esotericist?

AF: It lies, I'd say, in each individual's effort to eliminate the accidental and arrive at the essential. From then on, there is no longer any distinction between a true mystic and a true esotericist, but identity.

BB: René Guénon nevertheless denied this identity and emphasized the differences in perspective. For him, the mystic had not yet completely freed himself from individuality, whereas the "esotericist" had.

AF: In fact, Guénon saw a historical break around the time of the Renaissance. The word mysticism took on a new meaning, essentially religious, and therefore, for him, "exoteric," whereas previously its meaning had been linked to the mystery traditions and therefore to initiation. This new "mysticism" was his target. He saw it as a form of debasement and abandonment of full spirituality. From this point of view, he wasn't entirely wrong.

BB: So he was a bit right?

AF: Yes, I share this opinion, in the sense that, precisely from this change in historical climates, true spirituality has in fact lost something qualitatively, and has become "subjectivized" so to speak (hence the individuality from which the mystic would be unable to free himself). In fact, it's enough to read the texts of the great mystics of Christianity up to the 16th century and compare them with the prolific texts of the 19th century to see some significant differences. In particular, the language of the mystic has been transformed: from ineffable, audacious, and absolute, it has become quite emotional, morbid, and sentimental.

BB: It's still a somewhat caricatured discontinuity, closely linked to the particularities of a certain 19th-century mysticism.

AF: Yes, no doubt, and one should never generalize. Every era has had exceptions that confirm the rule. I'm thinking, for example, of a great saint like Thérèse of the Child Jesus and of the Holy Face, loved and venerated as far away as Asia. And she's not the only one!

BB: If we now turn to the relationship between mysticism and initiation, what would you say?

Mysticism or initiation?

AF: So… Perhaps we can say that mysticism is a form of initiatory experience, but then initiatory rites and practices have been abolished, annulled.

BB: "Indirect" graces are erased by direct, theophanic grace.

AF: Exactly, even if some have spoken of "cultural fashions" that could be re-editions of myth. That's what the mythologist Carl Kerenyi (1897–1973) thought: that the mythological machine is still at work. However, from my point of view, "the machine" is not a *Deus ex machina*, but a generous and far-sighted God, although this definition has little or nothing of the esoteric about it.

BB: In any case, we've clarified the relationship between mysticism and esotericism, and recognized that true esotericism necessarily has a mystical character. How would you conclude this interview?

AF: Hoping not to scandalize anyone, I'd like to say that, in my opinion, true esotericism is always religious, and if it isn't, it isn't esotericism. The vertical dimension of religion is, in my humble opinion, essential to true esotericism.

Chapter 8
Jewish Esotericism

Many esoteric traditions are linked to a particular religion. The originality of each tradition requires that the respective esotericism be discussed separately. Indeed, bridges or simple influences between religions—as illustrated by the Christian cabala, for example—are more a matter of history than esotericism per se.

BB: What can you say about Jewish esotericism?

AF: First of all, there's a lot of literature on the subject, perhaps even too much.

BB: What do you mean by that?

AF: When an esoteric tradition is too much in the public eye, it often means it's in the final phase of exhausting its initial momentum, or even going off course.

BB: We'll no doubt come back to such "deviation" phenomena in later discussions... I suggest we start by talking about its origins.

The origin: Merkavah

AF: Here again we have a problem, for what is generally called "Jewish esotericism" is almost exclusively identified with Kabbalah, which is said to have emerged around the 12th century and, if this is indeed the case, we would have to agree that it is more an abstruse concoction of thought than a true esotericism.

BB: Isn't it a bit harsh to so describe an enlightened and ingenious concept that is both mystical and speculative?

AF: I certainly agree with this: only highly refined minds could have constructed such a complex and coherent system. But the question is whether or not this extraordinary speculative construction has roots in the most ancient Judaism, and whether these roots sprang immediately from the ground or remained hidden and concealed for a thousand and five hundred years.

BB: Are there any "historical" elements that might provide clues?

AF: Certainly. At least as far as ancestral origin is concerned, it's the mysticism of the *Merkavah*, also known as the "mysticism of the chariot."

The Hebrew word *merkavah*, which translates into English as "chariot" and into Italian as "biga,"[1] derives from the r-k-b consonant root, meaning "to go up." References can be found above all in the famous book of the prophet Ezekiel, dating back to the 6th century BC and all too famous today.

BB: What do you mean?

AF: Because a certain pseudo-scientific literature, known as "paleoastronautics," has claimed that Ezekiel was abducted by extraterrestrials, and that the "vision of the chariot" was a trip in a spaceship![2]

BB: It's always amazing to see how certain things can be

---

[1] Typically Italian, *biga* is a technique for preparing dough (ciabatta, pizza) by pre-fermentation with brewer's yeast.

[2] The reference here is above all to the books by the Swiss mythographer and ufologist Erich von Däniken (1935–).

reinterpreted in rather grotesque ways by our contemporaries!

AF: Exactly! Whereas this "chariot" simply symbolized the prestige and supremacy enjoyed by rulers in ancient times. The "chariot" was in fact a sign of power that gave the one who rode it a clear superiority, including in combat. Then all this is transposed to a higher level, and the king's chariot becomes God's heavenly chariot, the chariot of fire, a celestial vehicle symbolizing "divine glory." Ezekiel describes it as a chariot, with shining wheels in motion, but he never actually calls it a "chariot."

BB: And then it all ended up being interpreted in an esoteric key?

Interpretation

AF: Exactly. This happened around the 3rd–4th century AD, but we can't be more precise. Not everything in this connection is in the Bible, because these doctrines were confidential, and only a few people had access to them. So those writing at that time, if they were aware of certain teachings, censored themselves.

BB: When we refer to Jewish esotericism, we have to bear in mind that the literature which speaks of it is only a reflection of it.

AF: Of course! And, as always, in my opinion.

BB: So what's the hidden part?

AF: In the initiatory experience itself. Doctrine is only a support, an echo, so to speak, of what the initiate has experienced and the degree of intensity and penetration of the realities lived and experienced.

BB: What can we say about these initiatory experiences from the texts we have?

AF: These texts describe "journeys to the beyond" (Guénon would have spoken of a kind of crossing into and participation in multiple states of being) in which the initiate contemplates the "heavenly chariot," which is no longer merely his vehicle, but, representing God, becomes the very goal of the initiatory journey.

BB: The sun's archetypal nocturnal journey...

AF: Exactly! What we call "natural phenomena" today was, for the ancients, symbolically something quite different. For the ancients, nature was overflowing with god(s). That's why it was still possible to contemplate its beauty as something divine. Analogies were continually developed between above and below, between Heaven and Earth, between the metacosm, the macrocosm, and the microcosm. And it's from the discovery of these analogies that many an esotericism has arisen.

BB: Esotericism reduced to philosophical or imaginative speculation...

AF: In a way, purely speculative esotericism is the "lapse" or translation into conceptual terms of an act that is at once reflective, imaginative, and cognitive on the one hand, and contemplative on the other. It is to the sum of these two things that we can give the name "sacred science," with everything in nature going back to its supernatural and sacred roots.

BB: The "marriage" of immanence and transcendence in philosophical terms.

AF: Why not? Returning to our Judaic esotericism and its "beginnings" among us in the form of "chariot mysticism," we can't fail to recognize elements belonging to other traditions too.

BB: "Loans" or rather "borrowings"…

AF: Sometimes, no doubt, but not usually. The idea of "borrowing" suggests "copying and pasting," to put it in modern language; yet we're talking about universal symbols that resonate everywhere and manifest themselves everywhere without anyone needing to import them from elsewhere. Even if Jung is no saint in my paradise, and whose theories, as Titus Burckhardt used to say, may have done even more damage than Freudianism, he clearly understood that symbols reside elsewhere (for him, in the unconscious) and that they manifest themselves everywhere, with strong analogies and symmetries. So there's no need to backdate anything; we should rather speak of an original model common to all traditions and esoterisms. However, it must be stressed that this pattern is in Heaven, not on Earth; it is outside of time.

BB: "Outside of time," so we can't speak of a primordial *Tradition.*

AF: If by "primordial" we mean a beginning, an origin in time, obviously not. Hence the confusion of some who place this "state" in prehistory and make Adam a kind of caveman enlightened by the Spirit (laughs). And all the conjectures about the alleged geographical location of Paradise on Earth have always derived from this erroneous idea. I don't know whether Guénon is responsible for this absurdity, because as far as I know, he spoke of it in timeless terms, and at most with references to sacred geography.

BB: It's an important subject to which we'll certainly return. As for this "chariot mysticism," in what other traditions is it found?

AF: The references are innumerable; let's mention, for example, the *vimana* of Hinduism, a term that, linguists tell us, has considerable affinities with the Hebrew *merkavah*. *Vimana* means at once "chariot of the gods," "boat," and "palace," in the sense of a sacred edifice, a temple, with the architectural reference to the "heavenly palace," which also exists in the Hebrew term.

BB: And when do we get to the Kabbalah?

About the Kabbalah

AF: I was just getting to that (laughs). The Kabbalah, officially from medieval times, is in fact, as I've tried to say, just a second stage in Jewish esotericism, let's say a re-edition of it, merely deepening and developing the themes of the "journey into the unknown" that the "mysticism of the chariot" had described so well symbolically.[3]

BB: The very term "Kabbalah" lends credence to this historical understanding, it seems.

AF: Kabbalah, cabbala, qabale, *qabbalah*—we can say it

---

[3] On the subject of Merkavah, we will relate here what was pointed out to us by a friend who is more expert on the Jewish faith: "The *Ma'asseh Merkavah* is a tradition not really occult but reserved for people of experience, linked in fact to the creation story; but also, in certain (Hasidic) traditions, the *merkavah* represents the three patriarchs (Abraham, Isaac, and Jacob), each embodying one of the three sephiroth *Hochmah*, *Binah*, and *Tipheret*, as part of the 'work of redemption' incumbent on every good Jew, every act of obedience to God's law making him a 'chariot,' for His glory."

any of these four ways—literally means "reception," "tradition." It's clear, then, that we're referring to something that hasn't been invented, but received. The question is: received and transmitted by whom? I think we have to imagine an oral tradition that has been perpetuated over the centuries; even historians can't rule it out, all the more so as many passages in the Bible suggest that it already existed from the time of the writing of the Holy Scriptures. Everyone talks about these "oral traditions," even Plato, and there's really no reason to doubt their existence.

BB: It's the classic pattern you were pointing out, "oral traditions" eventually receive an external "cover," namely that they are finally written down.

AF: Exactly.

BB: According to this idea, which also seems correct to me, that the origins of Kabbalah are lost in the mists of time essentially means that they go back to Adam. But what do scholars have to say about so-called "foreign" influences?

AF: Among the most famous and important scholars, even today, I would like to mention Gershom Scholem (1897–1982) and, above all, Moshe Idel (1947). Without excluding elements of exogenous origin, Idel maintains the presence of a strong Jewish matrix, reflected in a number of basic doctrines, such as speculations on divine names, the dual principle of mercy and rigor, messianism and so on.

BB: So what has Kabbalah added to the "mysticism of the chariot"?

AF: Without wishing to over-generalize or oversimplify, I'd say, essentially, the cosmogonic aspects; i.e., those dealing with the theme of the origin of the universe, and also of what it's tending towards, much more than the cosmological aspects—and dealing as well with the universe, but with reference to space, time, and matter. The "mysticism of the chariot" was precisely mystical, theosophical, and therefore fully esoteric and metaphysical, whereas the Kabbalah is more speculative and mysteriosophic.

BB: Can you put it another way?

AF: Let me simplify by saying that Kabbalah is a "science," a "sacred science" to be sure, but a science nonetheless. Its entire discourse on the mysticism of numbers and letters, which is fundamentally its core, is conducted with the rigor typical of a state of mind or mental structure, both mathematical and logical at the same time. And all the ensuing complications, which only an "initiate" can face and overcome, are there to prove it.

BB: Would you say that all speculations about angels, divine names, eschatological prophecies, etc., are also treated *ordine geometrico*?[4]

AF: Sometimes, but not always! Here, it's perhaps worth remembering that the sources of Kabbalah are countless, even if the absolute reference texts are only two in number: *Sepher Yetzirah* ("Book of Creation") and *Sepher ha-Zohar* ("Book of Splendor"), which—the latter especially—represent the compendium and "sum" of medieval Kabbalistic doctrines.

However, while searchable translations of these books exist, in my opinion they are very difficult for anyone to

---

[4] "Following geometric order": deductive demonstrations modeled on mathematical proofs.

tackle. These texts explain the allegorical and anagogical aspects of the Torah; but without being Jewish and knowing Hebrew, approaching them can be arduous, even for one of our biblical scholars, let alone a non-expert.

The kabbalistic method

BB: And from there it's a matter of moving from the theoretical to the practical!

AF: That's right! What's more, the practical aspect can certainly not be achieved without a guide, without a master, without the help of an expert. And even so, the work proposed is so vast that a lifetime would probably not suffice.

BB: How would you present the Kabbalistic method?

AF: Kabbalah admits a multitude of forces in the outpouring of divinity, expressed in the various divine names such as the ten Sephiroth.[5] Sephiroth is the Hebrew plural of sephirah, from the Hebrew verbal root *spr* (to count), and from this derives the usual meaning of "to enumerate," also rendered as "emanation." In reality, these are the creative powers of *En Sof,* found at the four levels (*Atzilut, Beriyah, Yetzirah, Assiyah*)[6] and communicating with each other.

BB: How does this concept fit in with Judaism's strong belief in the "oneness of God"?

AF: In reality, God's supreme oneness is maintained, but it is a oneness that is both immanent and transcendent. God

[5] See Appendix A.

[6] The four worlds or levels of existence: *Atzilut* = world of Emanation, divine thought; *Briya* = world of Creation, souls, separate entities; *Yetzirah* = world of Formation, angels; *Assiyah* = world of Action, of physical existence, furthest from the emanation of divine light.

"pours Himself" into the world and into things, but without any modifications in Him that compromise His unity. Your books on metaphysics shed light on these aspects of the divine...

BB: Let's stay with these ten Sephiroth. Why ten?

AF: Because ten is the number of totality. That's how it was with the Pythagoreans, and it's no coincidence that in the Bible it's also the number of the divine commandments. I'm only mentioning the numerology of the Kabbalah, as this would take us too far and would require a specific study which, to my knowledge, has not yet been undertaken.[7]

BB: Are you referring to gematria?

AF: Exactly. Numerical values are assigned to words written in Hebrew or even Aramaic, revealing the existence of a relationship between the two. But these methods are highly sophisticated and even difficult to explain without the proper mathematical knowledge.

BB: Yet these figures are essential to scriptural interpretation...

AF: I would even go so far as to say that they are of decisive importance. Perhaps we should simply recall that the Kabbalistic method of interpreting the Scriptures was taken up by the Fathers of the Christian Church and developed especially in the Middle Ages.

---

[7] To my knowledge, one of the few texts to approach the subject from an academic point of view is Kieren Barry's *The Greek Qabalah: Alphabetic Mysticism and Numerology in the Ancient World* (Weiser, 1999).

BB: Are you referring to the literal, allegorical, tropological (or moral), and anagogical[8] methods of the "four senses"?

AF: Yes, exactly! The "literal" meaning corresponds to the Hebrew *pechat* ("simple"), which is the primary meaning that can be reached with elementary reasoning; the "allegorical" meaning corresponds to *remez* ("allusions"); the "tropological" meaning to *derash* ("exposition"), which is the real exegesis; and, finally, the "anagogical" meaning corresponds to *sod* ("mystery"). With the latter, we penetrate the divine Wisdom (*Hokhmah*) hidden in the Scriptures. This is the mystical meaning, the esoteric "Wisdom of Tradition."

BB: These four senses also correspond to the four fundamental degrees of reality.

AF: Exactly. From bottom to top, or from earth to heaven: *Olam ha-Asiyah* (the "World of Facts"), *Olam ha-Yetsirah* (the "World of Formation"), *Olam ha-Beriyah* (the "World of Creation") and *Olam ha-Atsiluth* (the "World of Emanation").

BB: It's easy to see how complex these interpretations can be for anyone who isn't culturally and traditionally involved. Historically, what has become of this knowledge-wisdom?

Lurianic kabbalah, Frankism, Sabbatism

AF: Around the 12th century, important schools were established in the Provence, Germany, and Spain, which became hotbeds for the dissemination of Kabbalah. However, little by little, the speculative and conjectural aspects

---

[8] Anagogic means (potential or power for) elevation.

became more complex, taking precedence over the "mystical" and "esoteric" aspects, and this is how we arrive at the 15th and 16th centuries, with characters who are certainly charismatic, but also, in certain respects, dubious and controversial. Such is the case of Isaac Luria (1534–1572) and Sabbatai Zevi (1626–1676), both Turks, through whom the Kabbalah took a new course.

BB: In esoteric terms, was it a lapse or a gain?

AF: As for the Lurianic Kabbalah, the basis of the Polish Hasidism of Ba'al Shem Tov (1698–1760) in the 18th century, more than a gain; he endowed it with a new form of order that was more spiritual in the broadest sense, and more religious than esoteric or initiatory. Personally, I have a great deal of sympathy for this movement, which has inspired so many good people and has also produced excellent spiritual fruit over the years; I wouldn't have any trouble calling it evangelical in many respects. As for Sabbatai Zevi—who, among other things, converted to Islam and is considered by Jews to be a heretic—I suspect a polarity inversion and therefore a lapse. In this case, we are dealing with an intelligent form of Gnosticism, with paradoxical and even dangerous elements for the spiritual unity of the person. And the same can be said of the doctrines of a Jacob Joseph Frank (1726–1791).

BB: Don't you think that introducing Frankism and Sabbatism into "Jewish esotericism" is a mistake? After all, the real Kabbalists were the others. Why talk about heretics?

AF: Because in esoteric studies of the Kabbalah, these two characters are often brought into play, and it was right to warn the serious student of the low quality of their interpretations. The existence of these characters explains, among other things, why some people tend to confuse esotericism with heresy.

BB: I think that's a good thing. Is there anything else you'd like to add?

AF: Let me conclude by saying that Jewish esotericism is among the most complex to study and understand, and that this complexity is also due to its strongly religious connotations. By this I mean that it is not pure esotericism, but something in between, a meso-esotericism.

Chapter 9

Islamic Esotericism

Sufism is well known as the esoteric "side" of Islam. But is it the only Islamic esotericism? Does Sufism itself comprise just one branch? Aldo La Fata's insight should prove fascinating here.

BB: Does Islam, which emerged after Judaism and Christianity, offer a specific esotericism?

Of the Arabic language and Ibn 'Arabi

AF: First of all, as we all know, there are many different types of Islam, although when we think of this religion, we usually immediately think of the Arab world. Of course, Arabic is the liturgical language of Muslims, and their holy book, the Qur'an, is written in Arabic. But Arabic was and remains a language of Christian populations also, and Arabic script itself was a Christian invention. On the other hand, Arabic is related to Aramaic, the language in which Jesus himself probably spoke.

BB: Why is this premise about the Arabic language so important to the subject we're talking about? What is the relationship between the Arabic language and Islamic esotericism?

AF: This is because *'Ilm al-huruf,* or *risalat al-huruf,* the science of letters, plays a fundamental role. Ibn Arabi (1165–1240)—the most important master of Islamic esotericism, who can be considered, according to my personal classification, a "scholastic," but also a "father" of esotericism—

95

wrote extensively on the subject in his famous treatise *al-Futuhat al-makkiyya*, "The Illuminations of Mecca" (1203–1240). And, mind you: this scholar was Arabo-Andalusian.

BB: Ibn Arabi is not well regarded by Islamic orthodoxy…

AF: In fact, only members of the Wahhabi sect in Saudi Arabia are very critical of him; but at the popular level, 'Arabi is very much appreciated. In short, it's only the "fundamentalists" and "modernists" who criticize him, and I'd say, "with good reason!" It's those who are controversial and those who deviate from the right doctrine and the right path, and certainly not the admirers of the great mystic, who are in the majority.

BB: Would you say that Ibn Arabi is at the origin of Islamic esotericism or was he only a part of it?

AF: He too, four centuries after the Hegira, is a "link in the chain," i.e., he has precursors. However, as an esoteric intellectual, scholar, and writer, he is probably one of the greatest of all time.

Women in Islamic esotericism

I'd like to take this opportunity to debunk a cliché about Islam, according to which women play a marginal role. This is not the case at all. Women occupy an important place in Ibn Arabi's writings. And not only that! According to his own testimony, he was initiated by a young Iranian woman called Nizham, whose name means "Harmony" (obviously, an initiatory name). Then there was his close relationship with Fatima bint al-Muthannaan, an Andalusian Sufi, whose degree of spiritual elevation he admired.

BB: Can we say that there is also a feminine current of esotericism in Islam?

AF: No doubt. I'm also thinking of the great figure of Rabia al-Adawiyya (713/718–c. 801), a mystic who celebrated pure love, and who was centuries ahead of Saint Vincent de Paul's "Ladies of Charity."

BB: How important is the feminine element in Islamic esotericism?

AF: Any authentic esotericism, whether anthropologically or metaphysically speaking, can lack nothing. The feminine pole must have the same importance as the masculine pole, and this seems very obvious to me in the history of Islamic esotericism.

BB: It's clear that the search for God, as long as it's authentic, knows no gender discrimination.

AF: Yes, let's put it that way! (laughs). By the way, when in esotericism you find a preponderance of the male element, then there's definitely something wrong. It's a real discrimination criterion.

BB: Agreed. So far, we've talked about Islamic esotericism, but not yet about Sufism.

Islamic mysticism, Sufism or esotericism?

AF: Usually, we tend to identify Islamic mysticism with Sufism and esotericism in general, as if they were the same thing, when in reality they are not at all. They may converge towards similar ends, but the means are different. As for the word "Sufi" (*suf* in Arabic), there is no absolute certainty, but it seems certain that the word derives from "wool," from which the white tunic worn by Christian monks was made.

BB: So Sufism was born as a form of emulation of Christian monks?

AF: Emulation, but perhaps also rivalry: a kind of competition for perfection. If this were the case, however, we'd have to admit that Sufism would have been born tainted by religious exclusivism, i.e., with the claim to belong to a spiritual family superior to all others. The result would be an esotericism with denominational and ethnic connotations; in other words, a lesser esotericism.

BB: And do you think that's the case?

AF: Esotericism, as a form of "knowledge and love of God," must be an attestation of brotherhood towards all men without distinction. In my opinion, where Islamic esotericism has formally accentuated its religious exclusivism, it has *de facto* betrayed its mandate and disavowed its initiatory nature. And this eventuality has indeed occurred, in certain circumstances.

BB: However, this circumstance protected esotericism from persecution and kept it within the bounds of religious orthodoxy.

AF: This is true, thanks above all to the work of Abu Hamid al-Ghazali (1058–1111) who tried, I would say effectively, to "moderate" the "mystical" excesses and bring esotericism back into the fold of the Qur'anic magisterium.

BB: And al-Hallaj (c. 857–922) rather brought it out of it! (laughs).

AF: "The Khurasan Fool"! (laughs). Indeed, this character, to whom the great Islamologist Louis Massignon devoted almost his entire literary output, was the one who broke most with religious orthodoxy, and who ultimately found himself isolated. He professed the doctrine of *fana*: the annihilation of the ego in the divine, scandalizing many devout minds.

BB: Do you consider him an esotericist?

AF: Admittedly, he was a connoisseur of doctrines drawn from all over the world, including India. But I would define him more as a syncretist mystic, albeit one with great charisma. He had many disciples, so his word circulated, but I can't say how many of his teachings survived him. His execution and torture, which included floggings and amputations and made him very similar to our Jesus, were more political than religious.

BB: His story was a real turning point.

AF: Absolutely, after his condemnation, Sufism followed a more cautious path.

BB: Can you clarify this point: are Sufism and Islamic esotericism the same thing?

AF: Let's just say that their histories have often intersected and sometimes become so intertwined that they have become inseparable. Provided that esotericism is not seen as a philosophy, a doctrine, or a syncretism, but as the very essence of the doctrine, then this essence can also be reached through its own medium. The mandate of esotericism—including, of course, Islamic esotericism—is to grasp the essence, the heart of a doctrine, not only through symbolic and, thus, anagogic exegesis, but also through a process of identification, a true and proper assimilation of divine truth. The closer we come to this truth, the more we are in esotericism's sphere of influence.

BB: A great mystic can thus be considered a great initiate?

AF: Yes and no. As for the goal, yes, but the means are different. For Islam, God is everything and the creature must vanish before Him. The esotericist doesn't achieve this through a religious or mystical path, but by contemplating the wonders of nature and the cosmos according to a hierarchical scale that includes the visible and the invisible. For this reason, according to my idea of esotericism—and I stress that this is a perspective that has no scientific or historical character whatsoever—the great master of Islamic esotericism, or, as his students used to say, *al-shaykh al-akbar* ("the greatest master"), is Ibn Arabi more than either al-Ghazali or al-Hallaj were.

Duodeciman Shi'ism

BB: What about Duodeciman Shi'ism?

AF: Here we are confronted with a wonderful school with many points of connection to Christianity.

BB: And a great figure represents this school!

AF: Certainly: Suhrawardi (1155–1191)! His name means "inhabitant of Sohrevard," or "he who comes from Sohrevard." Elements drawn from Zoroastrian, Platonic, Islamic, Judeo-Christian, and even Hindu heritage resonate in his thinking. In appearance, then, a syncretism, but a highly enlightened syncretism, and thus, in a way, an esotericism in its own right. Henry Corbin (1903–1978) has written extensively on this subject, and it is worth referring those who wish to know more to his books.

BB: How would you sum up this master's teaching?

AF: Suhrawardi had developed the theme of a "human physiology" of light. But as we shall see, this was not just a "doctrine" or an abstruse philosophy. Behind this "doctrine" lay a rich symbolism, an experience of light. In short, esotericism resurfaces in its anthropological, cosmic, and divine aspects.

BB: Suhrawardi is therefore also a "father" of esotericism, isn't he?

AF: Father and scholastic, yes. And then, as a third radiating pole, we must also remember the often forgotten figure of Haydar Amoli (1320–1387 or 1408), also from Iran and author of numerous texts. With him, too, there is a link between Islamic doctrine and the theosophical wisdom of the ancient Persians. Many Imamite Sufi brotherhoods are descended from him.

BB: Would you say that these "fraternities," these brotherhoods, are esoteric organizations?

AF: Let's say in the 12ᵗʰ century, yes. But in fact the brotherhood was the path devised by Islamic orthodoxy to regiment esotericism. Aspirants then began to be overly numerous, and the need for a rule and a hierarchy became apparent. Hence the Arabic term *tariqa* (plural *turuq*) meaning "path," "way." Then it came about that each brotherhood, to attract the greatest number of adherents, ended up establishing its own "initiatory chain" (*silsila*).

BB: You talk about it as if it were a betrayal of esotericism.

AF: Yes, that's true. I'm not being critical, of course, but merely making an observation about the institutional character of this form of esotericism. This character has also ended up creating episodes of fanaticism among the adherents of the brotherhoods themselves. And as I've surely said many times before, fanaticism has nothing to do with esotericism. Secondly, it must be recognized that the practices and obligations of worship, as well as the spiritual path itself, bring much good fruit within these orders. There's no arguing with that.

Practices

BB: So what are these practices?

AF: First and foremost is *dhikr:* the most important and widespread practice, consisting of the constant repetition of certain short prayers, uttered both individually and collectively, accompanied by body movements. Then there's listening to the sung Qur'an, mystical poems, or music, with or without dance.

BB: This brings us to Rumi and the whirling dervishes.

AF: Absolutely; and it's a shame that dervishes have been reduced to a folkloric, theatrical phenomenon, and that Rumi has become a trivial literary phenomenon. There's a real esotericism in both. For both, reality is a symbol to be contemplated, it's true reality.

BB: Is there a text by Rumi you'd like to recommend?

AF: Certainly, the Persian poem the *Masnavi,* still better known as *Masnaviyi Manavi* ("Spiritual *Masnavi*").[1] It is a work that has been defined as a "Qur'an in the Persian language," and editions of it can be found in almost every language.

BB: I'm sure there's a lot more I could say, but I think we'd better call it a day.

---

[1] Six books containing 424 allegorical stories on the condition of man seeking God.

Chapter 10
Christian Esotericism

With two millennia of Christianity in Europe, there is a pleth-ora of associated esotericism. How do you find your way through them, and understand their diversity as well as their possible unity? There are differences between Catholic and Orthodox esotericism, but is a Protestant esotericism possible? These are just a few of the questions that Aldo La Fata felt deserved a little enlightenment.

BB: The first question I'd like to ask you is this: did Christian esotericism really exist, or is it a "ruminating hare"?[1] (laughs)

Christian esotericism or Gnosticism?

AF: (laughs) I wouldn't want to gainsay Zoccatelli, who is a serious scholar whom I respect and to whom we owe truly fundamental historical studies on the great symbolist and Christian iconographer Louis Charbonneau-Lassay (1871–1946), but in fact, the hare is a ruminant, albeit an atypical one. And then, may I reply that yes, a Christian esotericism has existed and may still exist, albeit atypically.

BB: Atypical in what way?

---

[1] In reference to a work by Zoccatelli, an Italian sociologist and essayist, deputy director of Turin's Center for Studies on New Religions: *Le Lièvre qui rumine. Autour de René Guénon, Louis Charbonneau-Lassay et la Fraternité du Paraclet* (Archè Milano, 1999).

AF: Firstly, because it is historically more difficult to identify, and secondly, because the Catholic Church has made it the equivalent of heresy.

BB: Are you referring to "Christian Gnosticism"?

AF: Yes, that's right. We've already talked about this, but I'd like to reiterate here that Gnosticism, insofar as it was in competition with the Church, was never esotericism, either *de jure* or *de facto*. Esotericism is not another religion, pseudo-religion, or counter-religion. True esotericism has never set out to oppose a traditional religion, even dialectically. In short, esotericism has never been a sect or even, on a theoretical level, an ideology. These things are the exact opposite of esotericism.

BB: This is to say that the Cathars, Albigensians, Bogomils, Paulicians, Arians, Manichaeans, etc., are not esoteric organizations?

AF: Absolutely not! But, as they say, I wouldn't want to throw the baby out with the bathwater. In all these movements, there were undoubtedly esoteric aspects, but detached from their original context and mixed with spurious elements from the most diverse sources. All this can certainly be called religious syncretism.

Syncretism

BB: Syncretism was once a fad and it seems to have never really gone out of fashion…

AF: That's right! Our fine scholar Elemire Zolla has exalted it and made it almost a manifesto in his books, but my impression is that syncretism is not very different from dogmatism when it becomes radicalized, and that its esoteric or mystical relativism is not very different from fideistic or rationalist relativism. It's a *melting pot*, the result of which is the coexistence of elements so disparate that, in the end, one cancels out the other. So the fact that someone manages to profit from all this, even spiritually, doesn't mean it's good in itself.

BB: I understand. Can you give historical examples of religious syncretism in Christianity, in addition to the Gnosticisms of all kinds already mentioned?

AF: Certainly! The champion of this syncretistic esotericism was undoubtedly Pico della Mirandola (1463–1494). In this authentic Renaissance genius, Orphism, Pythagoreanism, Chaldeanism, Hermeticism, Neoplatonism, etc. converged into a whole. But the end result was that very little Christianity remained. And it was this emptying out of the Christian element, which accompanied its reduction from esotericism to magic, passing—smuggled in—for the *scientia naturalis*,[2] which was disquieting. Even reference to what was "secret" had an equivocal connotation for him. Nevertheless, he remains a giant, and is widely believed to have died a Christian. Consequently, I certainly don't wish to criticize either his work or his thought, but only to point out that Pico della Mirandola has never represented Christian esotericism.

An Essene Jesus?

BB: Let's go straight to the *medias res*.[3] What do you think of the hypothesis of an Essene Jesus?

---

[2] He was a pupil of the philosopher and occultist Marsilio Ficino (1433–1499).

[3] "In the middle of the thing (in the center of the dispute)"; cf. Horace, *Ars poetica*, v. 148.

AF: This hypothesis of a "great initiate" Jesus appeared in the 19th century under the imaginative pen of Édouard Schuré (1841–1929). Later, especially after the famous archaeological discoveries of the Qumran site, the hypothesis of an Essene Jesus began to spread. The Essenes harkened back to the Pythagoreans and also the *thiasoi*, or cultic units of the Orphic mysteries. There is also talk of a related community, that of the Therapeutae,[4] and someone has even proposed the hypothesis of a derivation from *Theravada* Buddhism, also called *Theraputra* or *Theraputta*, a word apparently similar to that of Therapeutic.[5]

BB: Are these hypotheses credible?

AF: There are many supporting documents, including historical and documentary ones, but it doesn't seem to me that there is anything certain. There are undoubtedly affinities between the teachings of Jesus and those promoted by these fraternities, but to speak of a real derivation or filiation is a hypothesis rejected by most scholars, even non-Christians. Jesus may have been somehow linked to these esoteric organizations at some point, and if so, he distanced himself from them.

BB: Still, the Essenes and the Therapeutae were initiatory organizations, right?

AF: Yes, they certainly were, but probably already imbued

[4] It was Philo of Alexandria who likened this Hellenized Jewish sect to the Essenes (cf. his *De Vita Contemplativa*).

[5] Cf. Pier Tulip, *Gesù. Un mito solare. Esegesi allegorica dei Vangeli* [Jesus, a Solar Myth, Allegorical Exegesis of the Gospels] (Rome: Formamentis, 2019). The author takes up the theses of historian Henry Hart Milman (1768–1868), who was convinced that the Therapeutae were descended from the "contemplative and indolent fraternities" of India.

with errors of all kinds, such as excessive zeal which, as I've already said, is a very unesoteric attitude and an indicator of spiritual immaturity. Similarly, deviant esotericists were very much attacked by Jesus: the Pharisees.

BB: Do you think the Pharisees are esotericists?

AF: Of course. *Perushim* (Greek *pharisaioi*) means "separated" in Hebrew. They were the ultra-observers of the Mosaic Law. This was already an excess, then they corrupted themselves by becoming part of the *Sanhedrin*, a kind of Jewish Senate. They thus became a "power group." Hence their being singled out by Jesus.

BB: As you said, sectarianism in all its forms is the negation of esotericism.

AF: Worse than negation! I'd say it's the *inversion* of esotericism.

BB: A question comes to mind: what connection do you see between the figure of Jesus and esotericism?

Jesus and esotericism

AF: Jesus is a turning point, marking the line between a before and an after. Before Jesus, esotericism conveyed the purity of doctrine, the link with the highest spiritual realities and the means to reach them. After Jesus, esotericism underwent a process of vertical fall, collapse, loss of center, but also of rebirth to a new life. A new life, moreover, which, when given, has always been given in Christ and never outside or against him. This is the supreme distinction. Esotericism that fails to recognize the *Logos*, or confuses it with the *logoi*, is a false esotericism. True esotericism is that which understands the *logoi* and rises to the *Logos*.

BB: Of course, this *Logos* you speak of is Christ the Word of God made man.

AF: Of course it is! However, the Church tends to limit it to its identity-based horizon, whereas the esoteric perspective sees it in a wider horizon. The divine dimension cannot be circumscribed by anything, not even by religion, and religion's task is rather to give everyone the tools to go further. That's why it was "founded" not to imprison men, but to free them from prisons.

BB: Doesn't this discourse risk relativizing religion and the religions?

AF: It's the other way around! Religion is only relativized if it's seen as a beautiful closed chest. We know that the chest contains priceless treasures, but we're prevented from taking advantage of them. I believe that with Vatican II, the Church invited all Christians to open this chest wide and enjoy its treasures. And it's for this reason that today we can speak freely about Christian esotericism without incurring serious disciplinary sanctions or being branded heretics.

BB: I don't want to seem insistent (laughs), but you still haven't given any precise clues as to where Christian esotericism fits in.

AF: I didn't give any because this Christian esotericism doesn't have a precise location! (laughs). I'm joking, but not that much. I don't want to sound too reticent, but in fact we're dealing with something very elusive. When it comes to clues, we're missing, as the English say, the *smoking gun*.

BB: So what can you tell us about it?

AF: I said that Jesus was not a "great initiate," but, at the risk of seeming to contradict myself, I'll say that Jesus was also the greatest initiate in all known history. Not only am I not taking away any of the qualities attributed to him by the Church, I'm adding this one. And, since according to the school of Pythagoras (laughs), we're not afraid to add to it, I'll say that Jesus is even the pole of esotericism and initiation.

BB: An esotericist *a deo* and *ex nihilo*, with no connection to an esoteric tradition.

AF: Being the pole, he didn't need it. However, he was baptized by the Baptist, so he received an initiation.

BB: It was even a theophany.[6]

AF: Of course! But there was also the "presentation in the Temple" (cf. Luke 2:22–23), when he was dedicated to the Lord according to Jewish law. (Lev. 12, Exod. 13:12–15) The truth is that no initiation is exclusive. Initiations can easily be added. As you know, you can be a Sufi and a Freemason at the same time! (laughs). I mean, Jesus can be considered an initiate, and what happened at Pentecost, for example, could only have happened because Jesus was the pole of all initiation.

BB: There we have the treasure chest! So you see in early Christianity a genuine initiatory nature. But has this nature, as Guénon would have it for example, been lost?

AF: Let's say it's hidden. Around Christ gathered not only the so-called "popular masses," but also favorite disciples such as St Peter, St James and St John, the "secret disciples"

---

[6] "Heaven opened, and the Holy Spirit descended upon him in bodily form, like a dove, and from heaven there came a voice: 'You are my beloved Son: in you I am well pleased.'" (Luke 3:22)

such as Nicodemus, Joseph of Arimathea, Lazarus, and the sisters Mary and Martha, etc., who can be arranged in concentric circles.

BB: I bet you don't include the Church of John! (laughs).

AF: Indeed, if I spoke of a Church of John, so dear to Protestants, an invisible Church, parallel to the visible Church of Peter, you would have reason to laugh or smile, but I will not speak of this "secret structure," this *Secret Intelligence Service* or Intelligence in the service of His Majesty Jesus Christ (laughs). No, I'd rather talk about St John as "the one the Lord loved" (John 13:23; 19:26; 20:2; 21:7, 20), and of the fact that Jesus spoke in parables—the explanation of parables taking place in private: "To you it has been given to know the mysteries of the kingdom of God, but to others it is given in parables, so that they may see without seeing and hear without hearing." (Luke 8:10)

Esotericism and exotericism

BB: Fair enough, but there are just as many passages in the Gospels that show a Christian revelation "for all," what some would call "exotericism."

AF: That's right too. A good explanation can be found in Pavel Aleksandrovich Florensky (1882–1937), one of the most significant and surprising figures in Russian religious thought. In his 1914 masterpiece *The Pillar and Ground of the Truth. An Essay in Orthodox Theodicy in Twelve Letters*, he observes that exotericism and esotericism are reconcilable in the most intimate Christian life, and only there.[7]

[7] Trans. Boris Jakim (Princeton: Princeton University Press, 1997), 301.

BB: As Jean Borella has also shown, this means that, in Christianity, esotericism and exotericism are inseparable.

AF: Indeed, it can be seen in this way. Exotericism could be a kind of testing ground which, when fully experienced, provides access to a higher level of consciousness. There would then be no need to postulate the existence of two Churches, or even two complementary paths, but one and only one, within which it is possible to travel the entire path to the supreme goal.

BB: Why, then, have there been explicit Christian esotericisms whose historical existence is undeniable? How can we resolve this contradiction?

AF: I believe that Christian esotericism has never needed to establish itself as such, but has manifested itself in the form of religious exotericism. Religious exotericism was aware of it until a certain historical moment, then forgot about it to the point of rejecting and denying it. I'm thinking of Silvano Panunzio's formula: exoterism as the esoterism of esoterism. Not having any institutional character, Christian esotericism can always re-emerge, because its existence is guaranteed by the relationship between center and periphery, by the hierarchical and philarchic relationship of its members, organized not in linear succession, but in dynamic, interwoven concentric circles.

Christian esotericism and Freemasonry

BB: That's very convincing. But then how do you explain the Knights Templar, the Faithful of Love (*Fideli d'Amore*), the Compagnonnage, Freemasonry, and the relationships established by the clergy itself with such organizations?

AF: The task of these organizations was to complement

and support true esotericism. Anyone who has entered the field of action of these organizations and has been co-opted and affiliated with them at some point, or even at the end of a highly complex initiatory journey, then returns to the simplicity of faith, but returns transformed.

BB: So these organizations are not a detour on the road?

AF: Only when they are considered in their own right, as autonomous bodies independent of traditional religion. Their extinction is linked to their claimed autonomy and their contamination by power; a bit like what happened to the Pharisees. This explains the tragic end of the Knights Templar, and also the disappearance of the Rosicrucians, or their "flight" to the East. In the case of Freemasonry and the Compagnonnage, it was the move from the operative to the speculative that doomed them.

BB: Do we have to discredit all this Christian esotericism?

AF: Certainly not, but what remains of these organizations today? Little more than nothing; a residue from which it's best to distance oneself. However, certain symbols and teachings are still present, and anyone who becomes aware of them can benefit from them in one way or another. Freemasonry, for example, can be described as an ark of symbols, and it's true! Joining it, becoming part of it, is another matter. Here we are coming into contact with a world that for three hundred years has been hostile to Catholicism, even if a certain number of ecclesiastics have been and still are part of it. In addition, there has been a serious contamination by the occultism of the 18th and 19th centuries.

BB: Should we exclude the possibility that a Catholic can also be a Freemason?

AF: I don't want to rule it out completely. Maybe it will even become possible, but as long as the negative opinion of the Church remains, I don't think it's appropriate.

Christian esotericism and Neo-Platonism

BB: You mentioned a few Christian esotericists. We spoke of the ones that are best known to the general public and sometimes smack of heresy. Have there been others, perhaps more orthodox?

AF: Christianity was influenced, and I would even say irradiated, by the Neoplatonist movement. Above all, its theology was strongly influenced by it. Even today, Neoplatonism has had and still has illustrious representatives. I'm thinking of Vittorio Mathieu (1923–2020), Werner Beierwaltes (1931–2019), Pietro Prini (1915–2008), Giovanni Reale (1931–2014) and many others, including Jean Borella (1930–).

BB: However, we're talking, so to say, about professional philosophers, even metaphysicians, not esotericists as such.

AF: I'd say we're talking about a community of people inspired by one of esotericism's greatest points of reference. As I see it, Christian esotericism is made up of concentric circles, and some philosophers and theologians are also part of it, sometimes perhaps unconsciously, but they too make their contribution to the cause of esotericism. It's not just an attraction to a certain form of thought, but, to a certain extent, it's also a form of brotherhood and spiritual communion. They have entered this karst river that has been flowing since the dawn of time.

BB: To use your categories again, should we talk about scholasticism or scholastics?

AF: I'd say syntonic scholasticism, because there's also dystonic scholasticism.

BB: A complementary subdivision?

AF: Yes, this points to the existence of a category of people akin to those defined as "grammarians" at the Alexandrian school in Egypt. Grammarians were scholars involved in the restoration, reading, explanation, and interpretation of classical texts. In short, they were the scholars—we'd call them "literary critics" today—who played the role of scholarly but "syntonic" link between wisdom and knowledge. Dystonic scholars, on the other hand, are those who lack, as Guénon would have said, "intellectual qualifications," and are unable to make the truth resonate in the things they write about.

BB: A distinction that may come in handy later on. To sum up, Catholic esotericism, from a historical point of view, includes all the neo-Platonist currents, the Templars, the Faithful of Love, Christian Hermeticism, the Christian cabala, the medieval guilds, Rhenish mysticism and... what else?

AF: Definitely the "cenacle" around Paray-Le-Monial. In this monastery lived the mystic Saint Marguerite Mary Alacoque (1647–1690), a Christian nun and mystic canonized by Pope Benedict XV in 1920, and to whom we owe the cult and devotion to the Sacred Heart of Jesus. Various "esoteric" and pseudo-esoteric realities were subsequently linked to this cult and charismatic experience, such as the movement linked to the "Atlantide" association of Paul Le Cour (1871–1954), the magazine *Regnabit* by Father Félix Anizan (1878–1944), which also featured contributions from René Guénon and Louis Charbonneau-Lassay (1871–

1946), and today's *Contrelittérature* by our friend Alain San-tacreu (1950–), which has attempted to return to this theme for some time.

BB: There's so much to talk about! And even though we've essentially stayed within the sphere of Latin Catholicism until now, can you say a few words about Northern Protestantism and Eastern Orthodoxy?

Esotericism and Protestantism

AF: Of course! There's the connection between Rosicrucianism and Lutheranism: the distinguishing symbol of the Rosicrucians was Luther's coat of arms. However, it's very likely that these Rosicrucians weren't the real Rosicrucians, but merely an organization that eventually appropriated the name. At least, this was the idea of Guénon, who also claimed a link with Islamic esotericism after the destruction of the Order of the Temple. But this is a question about which we can say very little, as there are no precise historical traces.

BB: Has Protestantism been influenced by a false esotericism?

AF: Personally, I think so. Luther's hatred of St Thomas Aquinas and Dionysius the Areopagite argues in favor of this, as does his specific rejection of the *analogia entis*, with anthropological consequences that reveal an important break with true esotericism. Theobald Beer (1902–2000) has attempted to demonstrate, with good arguments, that in many respects Luther's thought takes up themes from Hermeticism. But then we have to ask: what is this Hermeticism? Certainly a counterfeit.

BB: Some would say it's the same thing (laughs).

AF: (laughs). Remaining in the context of Protestantism, the thesis of English historian Francis Young[8] seems interesting: many esoteric texts preserved in monasteries—the famous "monastic treasure"—began to circulate just after the Protestant Reformation, when many orders were dissolved and convents closed. It was the circulation of these texts that encouraged the birth of occultism. I don't know if this actually happened, but it seems an interesting lead.

Esotericism and Orthodoxy

BB: And what can you say about hesychasm? Do you see it as esoteric?

AF: An esotericism with its own characteristics. Hesychasts (the term derives from the Greek *hesychasmos*, from *hesychia*, which is sometimes translated as "silence," calm, peace, tranquility, etc.) practice the so-called "Jesus prayer" or "prayer of the heart," which consists in endlessly repeating the formula, modulated to the rhythm of the breath, "Lord Jesus Christ, son of God, have mercy on me a sinner" (Greek: *Kyrie Iesou Christe, Yie tou Theou, Eleison me ton amartalon*).

BB: How old is this technique?

AF: Historically it goes back to St Evagrius of Pontus (4th century), but it's not clear whether this is "flour from his own bag" or whether he borrowed it from others. In this respect, there are various hypotheses, but the link with Islamic esotericism, Sufism, and even Indian yoga techniques seems established. Metropolitan Anthony (Bloom)

---

[8] Francis Young, "The Dissolution of the Monasteries and the Democratisation of Magic in Post-Reformation England," *Religions*, 2019, Vol. 10, no. 4, 1–10.

of Sourozh (1914–2003), one of the most authoritative spiritual figures of the Christian East in the last century, spoke of "Christian yoga"[9] in one of his famous little books. In any case, it was on Mount Athos that the practice received a decisive boost thanks to the work of St Gregory Palamas (1296–1359) and, in the centuries that followed, especially through the famous anthology of spiritual writings known as the *Philokalia.*

BB: Not forgetting the famous *Tales of a Russian Pilgrim*!

AF: Without a doubt, a fundamental text!

BB: What about the author?

AF: Not much is known. The origin of the *Tales* is unknown, except for being written in the 19th century. We know for certain that the first edition of the work was published in Kazan (Russia) in 1881 under the title *Candid Tales of a Pilgrim to his Spiritual Father.* The protagonist is a pilgrim who crosses the vast spaces of Ukraine and Russia with only the Bible and dry bread. During a liturgical celebration, the pilgrim is struck by a reference to St Paul's exhortation to "pray without ceasing" (1 Tim. 5:17), and later meets a master (*staretz* in Russian) who teaches him the "prayer of the heart." It's a beautiful and touching text, which has become one of the world's most widely read classics of Christian spirituality.

BB: You mentioned Gregory Palamas and Evagrius of Pontus. Can they be considered as the "fathers" of Christian esotericism?

---

[9] *L'esicasmo, yoga cristiano, i centri sottili dell'essere umano e la Preghiera segreta del Monte Athos* [Hesychasm, Christian yoga, the subtle centers of the human being and the secret prayer of Mount Athos] (Naples: G. Rocco, 1955).

AF: I'd say that, in a way, they are, as is the anonymous author of *The Pilgrim*. But, as I've tried to say, classifications only serve to give us an idea of what we're talking about, but we can't and shouldn't categorize too much. Hesychasm is indissociable from the religious dimension, and if you don't understand this, you run the risk of making it into something it isn't.

BB: I think you're right. Regretfully, I think we have to stop here, as far as Christian esotericism is concerned.

AF: I think so too; doing ten volumes was not our intention! (laughs). However, one last necessary reference I'd like to make is that the Latin West also has its own prayer of the heart, better known as "cordial prayer," "pure prayer of the heart," "prayer of the presence of God," or "prayer of silence," etc., and whose reference texts are above all *L'Oratoire du Cœur* [*Oratory of the Heart*] by Canon Maurice Le Gall de Kerdu (1633–1694), published in 1670, and the *Traité de la Prière du Cœur* [*Treatise on the Prayer of the Heart*] by the Jesuit Jean-Pierre de Caussade (1675–1751). Two studies have appeared on this subject, which I personally consider fundamental, even essential: *L'oraison cordiale, une tradition catholique de l'hésychasme* [Cordial Prayer, a Catholic Hesychastic Tradition] by Jean-Marc Boudier (L'Harmattan, 2013) and *La fatica del cuore. saggio sull'ascesi esicasta* [*Effort of the Heart. Essay on Hesychast Asceticism*] by Enrico Montanari (Jaca, 2003).[10]

---

[10] Discussion on this topic continues in his most recently published volume: *Un umile regalità. Percorsi dell'esicasmo in Occidente* [*A Humble Kingship. Hesychasm's Paths in the West*] (Mimesis, 2022).

Chapter 11

Hindu Esotericism

The influence of Hinduism on European esotericism is well known. What, intrinsically, is esotericism in Hinduism?

BB: The influence of Hinduism is well known, particularly in the formulations of Western metaphysics (René Guénon, Frithjof Schuon); it undoubtedly influenced Guénon in his esotericism of the "King of the World." However, the first question is: is there really a Hindu esotericism?

AF: This initial question immediately clarifies the terms of the problem. The truth is that when we talk about Hinduism, we enter a complexity that requires a change in our usual point of view. Paraphrasing the Gospel, I'd say that there's nothing in India that isn't in some way revealed or not kept secret, i.e., that isn't, in some way, made known to everyone,[1] which would rule out the existence of esotericism. However, a closer look reveals that things aren't exactly like that, and that the Hindu point of view can help us understand a great deal about what we Europeans call esotericism.

BB: Let's proceed!

Esotericism and ashrams

AF: I'll start with these ashrams, scattered all over India in their tens of thousands, which were once high places of

---

[1] "There is nothing hidden that should not be revealed, nor anything secret that should not be known." (Luke 12:2)

meditation and hermitage, immaculate homes for the irradiation of Hindu spirituality, but are now hotels and boarding schools, where millions of tourists flock to try to give meaning to their lives. Until the last century, it was possible to meet India's greatest ascetics, teachers, and seers: from Ramana Maharshi to Aurobindo to Ramakrishna to Vivekananda, from Swami Yogananda to Anandamayi, Sai Baba, and many others. Of course, much has been said about each of these figures—not necessarily always edifying—but at least these are names familiar to all.

BB: What relationship are you making between ashrams and esotericism?

AF: The Sanskrit noun *asrama* is a thematic nominal derivative of the root *sram*: "toil" and the prefix *a*, "towards." Consequently, an ashram is a place where one strives to achieve an ascetic and spiritual goal in a disciplined way. Of course they're not the equivalent of a European Masonic lodge (laughs), but, *broadly speaking*, you go there with similar aims and objectives. These places are centers of spiritual influence, like the great philosophical schools of antiquity we spoke of at the start of our interviews.

BB: It's true, these schools, and the masters, were the two poles of Western esotericism.

AF: Exactly! In India, the spiritual master (*guru* in Sanskrit) plays an almost more important role than the teachings he transmits. According to the interpretation of the late[2] *Advaya taraka Upanisad* (14–18), the term *guru* derives from the roots *gu* ("darkness") and *ru* ("to disappear"),

---

[2] Dated between 100 BC and AD 300, according to Gavin Dennis Flood (1950–).

meaning "one who disperses darkness." We're right at the heart of esotericism, which places the emphasis not so much on religious institution, tradition, or doctrine, but on the personal relationship between master and disciple.

BB: So where do traditions and doctrines fit in?

Rishis

AF: Tradition and doctrines play an important role, I'd even say a vital one, but without the mediation of recognized masters, they'd be nothing. At the root of Hindu tradition are the ancient "seers" (*rishis*). These are the true "revealers," with written codifications coming later.

BB: An oral tradition...

AF: Exactly. Knowledge passed on by word of mouth, or from heart to heart, sometimes without even speaking. The Sanskrit word for this is *shruti,* from the root *shru,* meaning "to listen." The superiority of orality combined with "unwritten doctrines" (*agrapha dogmata*), also supported by our own Plato, is the basis of esoteric teachings, which are not to be transmitted "through the press."

BB: How would you characterize the "orality" of traditional India?

AF: Not speeches, of course! (laughs). *Vac* (in Sanskrit and analogous to our *Logos*) was recognized as a creative, entirely spiritual, generative power. Before being a meaning, the word is a "sound." And it was with the modulation of voice sounds that knowledge was transmitted.

BB: Like the famous "aum" of certain yogic meditations.

AF: Yes. In the Vedas, for example, the importance of ritual is well understood, but its impeccable execution was closely linked to precise recitations of sacred formulas, sounds and words.

BB: All perfectly memorized.

AF: Yes, but in relation to memory as such. Memory has been the object of study and veneration since antiquity. Greek mythology personified it in the goddess Mnemosyne, daughter of Uranus and Gaia and mother of the Muses. Renaissance esotericism, with Raymond Lull, Giordano Bruno, and others, exalted it and used it for initiatory purposes: the famous "art of memory"! It's not just the physical fact of memorization; there's much more to it. Eliade understood this well enough to declare that "memory is the key to Paradise."[3]

BB: St Augustine in his *Confessions* also recognizes the value of memory. So, in your opinion, this aspect of the rite is esoteric?

AF: Exactly! The ritual practices, the science of sounds, the secret of sacrifice that the Vedas tell us about, were certainly not the heritage of everyone, and their very transmission took place outside communities, in the woods, in the deserts—in short, in uninhabited places, probably even in caves and ravines.

BB: You referred to "sacrifice." How important is its role in Hindu esotericism?

Hindu esotericism and sacrifice

AF: It has a central and fundamental role. For Hindus, world order depends on sacrifice, and this is perhaps one of

---

[3] Although the author has no exact recollection of the date and place of this lecture by the famous Romanian historian of religions in Italy, he nevertheless guarantees its authenticity.

the greatest "secrets" of esotericism. From the Latin *sacrifi-cium, sacer facere* explicitly means "to make sacred." Sacrifice is the intermediary between men and the gods. But the essence of sacrifice is known only to Brahmins, so it's not everyone's heritage. In this sense, we could say that the sacrificial rites of the Hindus were "esoteric" in nature.

BB: Rites and sacrifices were thus of paramount importance to the ancient Hindus, but then came the *Upanishads*. Are the *Upanishads*, like the Vedas, also the legacy of an esoteric tradition?

AF: I believe so insofar as these were priestly families who possessed and transmitted certain knowledge. The *Upanishads* are no exception. We know that in the beginning they were always read and meditated upon in secluded places, far from the crowds, for whom they were clearly not intended—a typically esoteric procedure. It was only later that schools were formed and the texts began to spread everywhere, giving rise to many different, sometimes even divergent, interpretations.

BB: At that point, to use the title of our book, are we dealing with "esotericism for everyone"?

Hindu esotericism and exotericism

AF: In a way, yes. Guénon felt that for India, the distinction between esotericism and exotericism was meaningless, both because of the absence of an institutional religion recognized by all, and because of the unitary nature of its traditions. But it was a Brahmanic idea that had a strong influence on him. And just as the Brahmin was the one whose task it was to "supervise" the proper execution of the sacrificial act, Guénon was the "overseer" of the purity of the esoteric tradition, or of its contemporary doctrinal expression.

BB: An interesting analogy, and one that would certainly be worth developing further, but let's stick to "Hindu esotericism." Since you speak of Brahmins as repositories of confidential knowledge that can only be passed on to a few, should we see the caste doctrine as a means of preventing certain knowledge from reaching the masses?

AF: I've never thought about it; or perhaps to some extent I have. The only thing certain is that the teaching of the Veda was reserved for those who had received a particular ritual initiation and therefore possessed the appropriate qualifications. The possibility of a "second birth"[4] was a prerogative, in the quadripartition of the caste system, only of the first three groups: priests (*brahmana*), warriors (*ksatriya*), and cultivator-artisans (*vaisya*), the so-called "servants" (*sudras*) being strictly excluded from it. Originally, it wasn't like this: before the priestly families were established, there were seers (*rishis*) and they are the true "fathers" of Hindu esotericism.

BB: Would you say that the Brahmins, like the Pharisees of Palestine, somehow betrayed the mandate received from the *rishis*?

About the Upanishads

AF: As long as the Brahmin families maintained the link with the sages, no! Obviously, something must have gone wrong and the continuity of the esoteric tradition must have been interrupted. But esotericism always rises from the ashes, and a new rebirth has taken place with the *Upan-*

[4] In this case, one would speak of *dvija* or the "twice-born."

ishads. These sacred texts in Sanskrit were composed from the 9th–8th century BC up to the 4th century BC.

BB: Esotericism never dies!

AF: And so it is! In my opinion, the path of knowledge traced by the *Upanishads* is linked to that of those original clairvoyant sages.

BB: Do you see any continuity between the two? We've talked about a kind of "internalization" of the idea of sacrifice…

AF: I would rather speak of *fulfillment,* as in the New Testament: "Do not think that I have come to abolish the law or the prophets; I have not come to abolish, but to fulfill." (Matt. 5:17)

BB: Added value, as it were.

AF: Yes, also because from a certain point onwards, we witness a degeneration of the ancient teachings. Eliade spoke in this regard of a "religious victory of the soil," eloquently witnessed in art, iconography, the rise of idolatrous cults of all kinds. What's more, at the same time as the *Upanishads* were being written down, yoga and *vedanta* were appearing.

BB: The *Upanishads* are therefore an esotericism.

AF: If we give the word *Upanishad* the meaning it's sometimes given, namely "private session" or "arcane, secret doctrine," then I'd say yes.

BB: But weren't the "masters"—*yogi* and *samnyasin*—at whose feet the disciple sat isolated beings who perhaps shared only a strong aspiration towards the Absolute and nothing else? Were they not initiates?

AF: Strictly speaking, the idea of an unbroken chain of initiates is not encountered until after the writing of the *Upanishads*, particularly within Buddhism and post-Christian Tantrism. But history only speaks of a visible hierarchy, whereas, as far as I'm concerned, there was also an invisible hierarchy, traces of which, for obvious reasons, will never be found, but to which a dense network of correspondences testifies and which cannot escape the trained eye. Of course, it's easy to believe that I see similarities where there are only coincidences...

BB: What counts here is, after all the studies you've done, what you think! To complete the picture, what about yoga and *vedanta*?

Vedas and vedanta

AF: *Vedanta* means "end of the Vedas" (*anta* = end), in the sense of sacred texts that are read, studied, and meditated upon last, while yoga is usually translated as "union," analogous to the Latin *iugum*: the yoke; and just as a yoke joins, yoga aims to join, to unite the individual self with its source, the universal Self, Brahman. The respective goals are not so different. The common goal is *moksha*, or "liberation." I'm obviously simplifying as much as possible, because in reality we'd have to go into a lot of detail, which we can't do here.

BB: Let's stick to the essentials, of course. What else might we add? For example, apart from the etymology mentioned, what relationship should we see between the *vedanta* and the Vedas?

AF: For Hindus, the Vedas are the equivalent of our Bible. We Christians say the Bible is the "Word of God" and the

Hindus say the Vedas are the "breath of Brahma," something "issuing from Him." In short, at the origin there is a direct inspiration of non-human origin—*apauruseya*[5]—and, in this sense, there is continuity and concordance between all Hindu scriptures. However, as with the *Upanishads*, the *vedanta* benefits from a supplemental grace—may the Hindus forgive me this Christian vocabulary (laughs)—which has taken the very spirituality of these peoples up a notch.

BB: How would you characterize this "jump in level"?

AF: A kind of "quantum leap," i.e., a sudden transition from one level of understanding and realization of reality and truth to a higher one. What had been ritual and worship was about to deviate into something magical and mechanical, so correctives like *vedanta* and yoga intervene. Here, we must remember that yoga as a "bodily technique" already existed and required, I'd say necessarily, an uninterrupted succession of masters and transmitters—and long before Patanjali therefore (2nd or 4th century BC) or whoever hides behind the name of the writer of the *yogasutrani*.

BB: Why don't you say a few words about yoga?

Esotericism and yoga

AF: This series of techniques involves the whole person and all his faculties without exception. Yoga bears witness to the fact that the ancients knew the secrets of the body and all the properties of the soul. And, in the case of yoga, one cannot speak of approximations as some would have it, but almost of an "exact science," capable, if applied and exe-

---

[5] Literally "non-human," in the sense of uncreated, revealed.

cuted impeccably, of transforming the practitioner's body, making it resemble that of a "god on earth." This is probably the other great arcana, along with that of "sacrifice," guarded by initiatic organizations of all times and places.

BB: A rather ineffable "secret," don't you think?

AF: Of course, a secret can neither be revealed or unveiled. Such a secret is not a mathematical formula or a coded message, which, by the way, no Enigma machine could ever decipher (laughs). As Father Dante would have said to this very point: "No one can understand who does not know it" (*Vita Nova*, chap. 26). You have to practice yoga to understand it, and the practice isn't for everyone, whatever some Westerners may think, who have often turned it into a kind of gymnastics.

BB: Would you say *vedanta* is superior to yoga?

AF: If yoga is one hundred percent esoteric, the *vedanta* is one thousand percent esoteric (laughs). Among other things, *vedanta* is a balm that minimizes the ever-present danger of deviation from yoga; a danger specifically feared in Patañjali's texts, which warn against the so-called "powers" that can be acquired through practice. Mental and psychic powers that can distract the practitioner from the goal and make him too attached to his own ego or to the powers to which progress would enable him to gain access. With *vedanta*, it's a question of turning attention away from the results obtained and of discernment within discernment, detaching oneself from everything and everyone in order to reach the nameless, formless, and indivisible Absolute.

BB: The famous spiritual guide to this path is Shri Adi Shankara.

Shankara

AF: Yes, the "Grand Master Shankara" (8th century), another "father" of esotericism. However, two other representatives of this "school" should not be overlooked: Ramanuja (11th–12th c.) and Madhvacarya (13th c.).

BB: Unfortunately, we can't talk about all three here, but what would you say is essential about Shankara's teachings?

AF: The central premise of Shankara's writings is the identity of the Self (Atman) and Brahman. Presented this way, it seems easy to understand, but thousands of pages have been written to explain it. Between his teaching and that of *Mahayana* Buddhism, there are undoubtedly points of connection, and thus the accusation made by other schools that he would be a "crypto-Buddhist"; but these accusations are resolutely rejected by his students. The atman is indeed identical with brahman, but, according to the *advaita vedanta,* they are not one, they are "not-two" (*advaita*). This is pure metaphysics, your domain.

BB: Okay, so what do you see as the relationship between esotericism and metaphysics?

AF: I think metaphysics is the culmination, the finish line in the double sense of "arrival" and "looking beyond."[6] There's a goal, but there's also a beyond, and we reach the goal precisely because we're able to look beyond. I believe that "in esotericism" we start from man and the cosmos, the visible and the invisible, in order to project ourselves even further, whereas in metaphysics the subject is alone with himself and has no need to project himself. He has

[6] In Italian, "finish line" is "traguardo," and "tra-guardare" expresses the idea of looking beyond.

already "arrived," and all he needs to do is become aware of it. Of course, this is just my idea of metaphysics.

BB: So you would say that an esotericism deprived of metaphysics would be a crippled esotericism, an acephalous esotericism?

AF: Yes, that's the most important lesson we can learn from Hinduism.

Chapter 12
Buddhist Esotericism

While Buddhism, on the face of it, places little emphasis on transcendence—as God—it is far from free of esotericism. Here's your chance to find out more.

BB: Buddhism is notoriously unconcerned with transcendence, or so many people think. However, there are Buddhist esotericisms, in a territory no less vast than that of Hinduism, and just as complex. So where do we start?

From the Buddha

AF: We must necessarily begin with its founder, the Buddha. Who was he really? The term Buddha, in Pali, means "one who knows or attains enlightenment." In other words, someone who, as it were, embodies a special transcendent quality within himself.

BB: Why have this personage and his teachings not been integrated into Hinduism?

AF: At first, it seems that the teachings of the Buddha were not considered to conform to the Brahmanic tradition. The *Sakyas* (perhaps that Iranian nomadic population attested to in the Eurasian steppe), from whom the Buddha is said to have originated, were considered by the Indians to be a "uncouth people," "of humble origin," and to this was added the aggravating circumstance that the great ascetic had not honored and paid homage to the Brahmins.

Buddhism or Hinduism?

BB: This explains why a great esotericist like René Guénon was able to regard Buddhism as an anti-traditional heresy for a time.

AF: Of course! Guénon had been a recipient of the Brahmanic tradition and had become its mouthpiece in the West. Then, as we know, the wise orientalist A. K. Coomaraswamy (1877–1947) managed to change his mind[1] by showing him the perfect orthodoxy of Buddhism.

BB: I understand that another Hindu scholar of good caliber such as Sarvepalli Radhakrishnan (1888–1975) also recognized that the teachings of the Buddha perfectly reflected the spirit of the *Upanishads* and that he had never intended to break away from Vedantism or found a new religion.

AF: That's right. And here, it's best not to go into the nonsensical and absurd accusation of atheism leveled against Buddhism by certain Western scholars, Christians by the way,[2] who sometimes seem to understand nothing of the spirit and doctrines of India.

BB: Indeed, it has been said that Buddha was a radical innovator and that there was a strong "subjectivist" component in his teachings, whereas Hinduism, almost to the contrary, was said to be all mystical and supra-subjective.

AF: Yes, these are examples of misguided and misleading interpretations to which, unfortunately, we Westerners often succumb. We think we understand others better than they do themselves, but this is not the case.

---

[1] On this subject, see A. K. Coomaraswamy, *Hinduism and Buddhism* (New York: Philosophical Library, 1943).

[2] Cf. "La filosofia indiana," *Asram Vidya* (Roma, 1998), vol. I, 344–58.

BB: Hence our Western misconceptions about Buddhist esotericism...

AF: (laughs) Orientalists tend to limit the discussion to a few sects, but in my opinion, the field is much broader. Not only is there a speculative part concerning doctrinal formulations, but also, the most important part, which is the practical part, including psycho-physical techniques borrowed mainly from Indian yoga.

BB: Esotericism may be a path, but it is no less based on a doctrine.

Buddhist esotericism

AF: In the case of Buddhist esotericism, I would say very precisely that it is first and foremost a path, but one that *also* has a doctrine, a supporting doctrine, as it were. And I'm not talking about a set of hypotheses, statements, and presuppositions, but an authentic "point of view" (*darshana* in Sanskrit), a particular view of reality or, as we say in German, a *Weltanschauung*, i.e., a "world view," "world image," or "world conception" that has profound anthropological, psychological, spiritual, and metaphysical implications. In short, something more than mere ideas born of abstract elucubrations and speculations, as some of us would be inclined to believe.

BB: But can we really say that Buddhist esotericism is yoga?

AF: I believe so, but an essential, practical, and effective form of yoga which consists of that meditative discipline (*dhyana, jñana*) which produced awakening, enlightenment in the Buddha. Without this technique, which constitutes the essence of early Buddhism, all subsequent developments would not be understood. When we speak of the Buddha's strictly ascetic orientation, we're talking about this practice which, as already mentioned, has historical roots that are lost in the mists of time.

BB: Did the later institution of Buddhist monasticism retain its esoteric component?

AF: Monasticism is, in my opinion—and as contradictory as it may seem to some—an esoteric public and religious institution. Even so is Christian monasticism, if you look closely, with all the distinct instances we can't go into here.

BB: However, doesn't the absence of hierarchies within these communities rather mark a break with esotericism? Wouldn't you say that esotericism is the prerogative of the few, and that not everyone has access to it?

AF: Certainly, but I'd say that, in itself, the criterion for selecting monks was in fact "aristocratic," and therefore, in this case, esoteric. Buddha's disciples were called "nobles" (*arya*).

BB: How would you sum up the principle of Buddhist meditation?

Buddhist meditation

AF: Essentially, it's a matter of stopping the incessant flow of thoughts. To achieve this, attention is focused on one of the Four Noble Truths (*catvari aryasatyani*): suffering, the cause or origin of suffering, the end of suffering, the Way out of suffering. When the deeper meaning of one of these truths was sensed, a kind of enlightening identification occurred in the meditator.

BB: Apart from meditation, do you know of any other "secret" practices?

AF: A wide range of practices has developed over time. Each school and sect created its own. And, of course, these highly subtle and refined techniques required guidance and initiation, without which results could hardly have been achieved.

BB: Risk of paltry results and possible deviations…

AF: Quite right. Taming movements of the soul such as anger or fear is a very complicated and risky business, as our psychologists well know. You really go down deep inside yourself and then it's not certain you can come back up. Hence the importance of teachers, discipline, and ethics, as well as the importance of a human community of reference (the *samgha* or *sangha*) to which we have duties and responsibilities.

BB: This is how Buddhism became a religion in every respect, including this "duty" towards others. Consequently, the attribution of a "divine personality" to Buddha at a certain point in time is not really a deviation from the original message.

AF: I don't think so. The deification of the Buddha repatriated one of the central symbols of Hinduism: that of the "cosmic man" (the *Mahapurusha*), the macranthropos, which represents the middle ground between individual man and universal being. I find it to be the greatest archetype that can ever be conceived and contemplated, because all correspondences and analogies between the microcosm and the macrocosm depend on it in one way or another. The "real person" is cosmic man, the unreal is the individual self. This truth is not very different from what John the Baptist proclaims in the Gospels when he says: "He must increase, and I must decrease." (John 3:30)

BB: Is this the sense in which you read the doctrine of the *anatman* (*anatta* in Pali), which affirms the non-existence of the *atman?*

AF: And that's my belief too. Now, I couldn't tell you the precise source, perhaps the *majjhimanikayo*, but it's the Buddha himself who, in one of his discourses, says verbatim that *tathagata*,[3] the name by which he sometimes referred to himself, "is a real person."

BB: So that it is to misinterpretations of this doctrine, even misunderstandings, that we owe divisions and schisms within Buddhism?

AF: I think so, even if sometimes misleading interpretations can shed light on neglected aspects of the doctrine, which will have to come to light again. As I've said before, truth can also be found in error. But there are also proposals and perspectives that attempt to divert man from the right path and lead him to ruin.

BB: And there are, as everywhere else, in Buddhism.

Buddhist esotericism and tantrism

AF: Absolutely. There are certain dark tendencies, mostly magical or shamanic, in the worst sense of the word. Unfortunately, there are some even today in Tibet, and it's a shame to be associated with them! Some encourage commerce with demons, particularly in the context of Tantric Buddhism. Although the aim is to recognize these demons

---

[3] The term can be translated as "the one who has thus gone away" (*tatha-gata*) or "the one who has thus come back" (*tatha-agata*). This ambiguity is generally interpreted as intended, and the term translated as "the one who comes and goes in the same way (of all the Buddhas)."

as part of oneself and thus convert them into liberating energies, the risk of failing and being dominated by them is very high.

BB: However, when we speak of esoteric Buddhism, it is precisely Tantric Buddhism and the so-called *vajrayana* that we are referring to.[4]

AF: Absolutely. The Sanskrit term *vajra* (lit. diamond or lightning bolt), referred to in the name of this Buddhism, indicates the immobility, immutability, and authenticity of Ultimate Truth. The transparency of the diamond indicates that the enlightened mind is "limpid" and transparent like a diamond, or dazzling like lightning.

BB: It remains a "traditional" school.

AF: Absolutely, even if in my opinion it's a relapse into a form of extrinsic esotericism, where primitive Buddhism presented itself as an intrinsic esotericism.

BB: What do you mean by that?

AF: With Buddha we went straight to the point, without too many doctrinal flourishes or complex operational subtleties. Tantrism, on the other hand, is the apotheosis of arcane disciplines, containing all the components of an "external," institutional esotericism: initiation, secret teaching, the need for a spiritual guide (*guru*), chain of transmission, magical implications, etc. It was precisely against all this that Siddhattha Gotama revolted, because he saw them more as obstacles or hindrances, sometimes even traps, which would then be difficult to get rid of.

---

[4] The *vajrayana*, or Diamond Vehicle, derives in part from *Mahayana* Buddhism; it also contains elements of Hinduism (Kashmir Shaivism).

BB: Are you really saying that this "third turn of the Wheel of the Law or Dharma" would be a betrayal of the other two traditional paths of Buddhism, i.e., the Lesser and Greater Vehicle?

AF: In a way, of course, but not quite. In fact, I don't deny that the goal can also be achieved by following this path. And on the other hand, certain paths arise to meet the needs, temperament, and inclinations of certain individuals, even those who would be mentally and physically damaged and who would otherwise have no possibility of "freeing" themselves. And, on a positive note, we should add that the tantras are imbued with dynamic attitudes that avoid those inevitable and recurrent processes of fossilization of doctrine and methods. Constantly restarting the Dharma wheel basically also means this continuous renewal of Tradition. Rotation = renewal; Dharma = continuity.

BB: What would you like to say about Tantra?

AF: These are highly complex doctrines and methods that require flawless execution, on pain of failure. They require the initiation and guidance of an authentic master. In Tibet, tantric teaching is only given to highly selected candidates with more than proven qualifications.

BB: What kind of qualifications?

AF: Above all, physical, psychic, and mental aptitudes, without which certain concentration, visualization, and creative imagination exercises would be impossible to practice. Here too, a great deal of willpower and iron discipline are required, otherwise the desired results will not be achieved.

BB: What would you say about the practices of the various tantric schools known as "right-hand" and "left- hand"?

AF: There is a correspondence with Hindu Shaivite tantrism. In the West, these two terms have even come to designate two "esoteric" or "magical" paths, opposed according to the absence or presence of behavioral ethics. We then came to identify the "left-hand path" with black magic and the "right-hand path" with white magic. But these were expansions and misapplications introduced by the ambiguous Helena Petrovna Blavatsky (1831–1891). For Tantric Buddhism, these two paths simply refer to the use or non-use of the Creative Forces, Energies, or Powers (*Sakti* in Sanskrit) which, in their symbolic universe, have a "feminine" and sexual character. In certain secret Tantric rituals, this symbolism is embodied by a woman and staged. With the form of a sexual union, a degeneration of these practices cannot be ruled out.

BB: It's certainly a big leap: from the Buddha's apophatic and ascetic Buddhism to partly sexual rites!

AF: Seriously, let's say that Tantra brings us back to giving value to reality. Here again, it's a counterweight. For a time, Christianity held the body and nature in contempt, until St. Francis of Assisi put things in their proper place. Nature and the body can be adequate means for supreme spiritual realization. And, in fact, if you think about it, esotericism, in its purest manifestations, has always sought to value the body, the cosmos, the energies and wonders of nature. And certainly this was never either materialism or "libertinism."

BB: From this point of view, while there is sex in Tantra, there is no sexuality in the libidinal sense of the word.

AF: In fact, it's essentially a question of converting and reabsorbing these sexual energies, transmuting them into something else, and it's from this transformation that enlightenment can arise. In short, it's not about desire. On the other hand, as Nagarjuna, the greatest metaphysician of Buddhism, wrote: nirvana can also be defined as "perfect knowledge of phenomenal existence."[5]

BB: And what about the *kalacakra* tantra?

AF: *Kalacakra* (a hybrid and polysemous term, the Tibetan term as well) is usually translated as "wheel of time" and then comes to designate a series of tantric Buddhist yogic texts and methods.

BB: What would you say about these rites and methods?

Buddhist esotericism and mandalas

AF: As far as I know—because there has always been a degree of confidentiality surrounding certain practices, and not everything has been written down—the practice would be divided into two phases: in the first, the *tantrika*, through complex visualizations, transforms the world into a *mandala*[6] and identifies with a divinity, an expression of enlightened nature, thus abandoning the ordinary way of seeing oneself and the world; in the second phase, one works on the vital breaths and their circulation in the body, and completes in reality what in the first phase one has created through thought. I would exclude the possibility of success for these methods. The result of this highly complex

[5] "Samsara is in no way different from nirvana. Nirvana is no different from samsara. The boundaries of nirvana are the boundaries of samsara. There is no difference between these two." Nagarjuna, *Mula-madhyamaka-karika*, XXV, 19–20.

[6] A mystical diagram, or geometrical drawing, elaborated with different materials and used for ritual or meditative purposes in both Hinduism and Buddhism. See Giuseppe Tucci, *Theory and Practice of the Mandala* (London: Rider & Company, 1961).

practice is by no means guaranteed, and must be repeated countless times under the guidance of an expert master. The *mandala,* which is drawn from time to time and then destroyed, serves the purpose very well.

BB: What would you say about the mandala itself?

AF: It represents the disciple and his relationship with the phenomenal world, but also with the cosmos as a whole and with the being we are, with all its faculties. Drawing a mandala and meditating on it is like going through and experiencing several states of being. Tibetan tradition classifies mandalas into different categories: those made of colored powder, those painted on canvas, and those created through meditation. But the human body is also a mandala. Few people in the West are aware of this, but mandalas made of colored powders are intended for people whose consciousness is not highly developed. The rest of us, in short! (laughs)

BB: (laughs) And to conclude on the subject of "sexual" rituals?

AF: The initiate is led to a form of supreme, "still pleasure" that is precisely identified with *nirvana* itself. Ordinary pleasure has little to do with this supreme pleasure. Physical pleasure, it's true, leads the individual to experience a kind of ecstasy, a thrilling enjoyment, but it's still an ego that feels; whereas the state attained by the *tantrika* corresponds to a total union with the whole that can only belong to the supra-individual Self.

Practical esotericism: Zen

BB: To complete this brief approach to Buddhist esotericism, we should perhaps mention those schools of Japanese

Buddhism founded, according to tradition, by the legendary Indian monk Bodhidharma and known in the West as Zen. But what does the word Zen actually mean?

AF: This expression derives from the Chinese term *Chan*, which in turn is an interpretation of the Sanskrit term *dhyana* ("vision") which, in the teachings of the Buddha indicated the gradual states of consciousness leading to deep understanding and resulting from meditative concentration. This form of meditation was then exported to China and Japan, where it took on its own particular character, was tied to the specific character of these people.

BB: So Zen, in your opinion, is an esotericism?

AF: I'd say so. An almost pure, intrinsic esotericism like that of the Buddha. In fact, here too, we're talking about drawing directly on metaphysical experience. I say experience just to be clear, because in reality we should be talking about pure gnosis, a dazzling intuition, an understanding of reality in its entirety, and an actualization of one's Buddha nature.

BB: If, in the end, what counts is the practice of meditation and its results, then how do you explain the existence of so many schools?

AF: In fact, there are several schools of Zen Buddhism, but let's just say that, more or less, they all retain the centrality of meditation practice. Differentiation is achieved through other elements that are fairly typical of institutional esotericism, such as the transmission of the magisterial "lineage," the adoption of certain specific traditional texts, particular meditation techniques, certain rites and ceremonies, and so on.

BB: Would you say that this proliferation of schools represents an esoteric loss?

AF: A loss and a gain at the same time. A sign of weakness,
but also of strength. Esotericism is far more capable than
religion in the strict sense of the term of adapting and
assuming the most diverse forms.

Esoterisms of the Buddhisms
of the Lesser and Greater Vehicles

BB: Is this how you would also explain the transition of
Buddhism from the Lesser to the Greater Vehicle, from the
ideal of the *arath* (liberated one) to that of the *bodhisattva*?[7]

AF: I don't think these are two different "ideals," but, esoterically, a different reception and understanding of the
same ideal. The *arath* doesn't just work for himself, and the
bodhisattva doesn't just work for others. In every *arath* there
is a *bodhisattva* and in every *bodhisattva* an *artah*. Esoteric
spiritual reality never contradicts itself; man does, and very
often (laughs).

BB: (laughs) It's true! And you have to get used to living
with contradictions. Is there anything else you'd like to add?

AF: I don't know. These initial indications should suffice;
it's up to the reader to elaborate, if he wishes!

[7] The *bodhisattva* renounces supreme liberation out of compassion
and to save all other beings.

Chapter 13
Taoist Esotericism

The Far East, and China in particular, is no exception when it comes to esotericism—far from it. Its defining features are well known in terms of metaphysics; what about the associated esotericism?

BB: We've reviewed the esoterisms associated with the world's major religious traditions, both Western and Eastern, and now, to complete the picture, we need to tackle the complexity of Taoism. Thanks to Guénon and many others (Granet, Wieger, Matgioi,[1] Maspero, Kaltenmark, Robinet, Anne Cheng, Conche, Laurant, Laude, Pregadio, Sablé…), Taoism is not unknown in Europe, but what about the esotericism associated with it?

Esoteric, religious, ethical Taoism?

AF: You say "the complexity of Taoism," and indeed, it's a reality that's not easy for Westerners to understand. Fortunately, we have an abundance of literature on the subject that can facilitate our work. In Italy, we have the excellent work of the great Lionello Lanciotti (1925–2015), and I was fortunate in the past to know the orientalist Pio Filippani Ronconi (1920–2010), who had studied this tradition in depth. Let's just say that it's mainly from their studies that I've learned what little I know of Taoism, its methods and

[1] "The eye of day," pseudonym of Albert Puyou, Count de Pouvourville (1861–1939).

doctrines. Of course, I'm not forgetting the contributions of Marcel Granet, Henri Maspero, John Blofeld, and Albert de Pouvourville, to name but a few.

BB: All these scholars seem to agree in defining Taoism as a religion, an ethical system, a worldview, and an esotericism. Can you tell us a little about its founder?

From the "axial period"

AF: Apparently a very wise "Old Lord" (*Lao jun*). The name by which he is known worldwide is Laozi or Lao Tzu, which literally means "old child" or "young old man." Of course, we can only assume that this character really existed, as there is no irrefutable historical evidence about him either. The name is obviously an epithet, a heteronym, or even an "initiatory name." But the interesting thing is that his "personality" suddenly appears on the world stage along with those of Confucius (551–483), Pythagoras (540–480), Jina (d. 527), and Buddha (563–483).

BB: In the so-called "axial period" (German: *Achsenzeit*), as the philosopher Karl Jaspers (1883–1969) terms it.[2]

AF: Exactly! By "axial period," Jaspers meant the period between 800 and 200 BC, in which personalities of notable spiritual caliber appeared and changed the course of history. Jaspers also mentioned Zarathustra, Isaiah, Homer, Parmenides, Heraclitus, Plato, Aristotle, etc. According to the German philosopher, these figures changed man's way of thinking, i.e., we began to think thought. But I see something else, and something far more important.

---

[2] Cf. *The Origin and Goal of History*, trans. Michael Bullock (New York: Routledge, 1953).

BB: What would that be?

AF: An event of an enormous spiritual nature, a manifestation on earth of what I have called "the golden chain," some of whose extraordinary figures were so many luminous rings.

BB: And how do these figures relate to prior traditions?

AF: A very strong link, as always, but their role was to renew, i.e., to adapt tradition to the new needs of the times. In my opinion, we must take this trans-formation very seriously, if we are not to risk diminishing the role of these great figures in human history.

BB: As far as Taoism is concerned, what was the previous tradition that Laozi renewed?

The origins of Taoist esotericism

AF: It dates back to the legendary Chinese emperor Fuxi or Fu Hsi, to whom the famous *Book of Changes*, the *I Ching*, is attributed. Whether this character really existed, or rather, as Guénon thought, he was the symbol of an "intellectual function," doesn't really matter! In any case, what is reported in this extraordinary text is still no more than the transcription of a knowledge that precedes it, of an oral tradition about which we know very little. Clearly, the transition from oral to written tradition inevitably leads to impoverishment—not to mention hybridization and contamination with false beliefs, exogenous doctrines, and God knows what else.

BB: We mentioned the risk of syncretism.

AF: Exactly! In the prehistory of Chinese tradition, we also find bloody elements such as human sacrifice, which has unfortunately long marred the history of almost all known civilizations, with a few exceptions of course. But we mustn't lump everything together: societies founded on sacrificial practices and ritual murder are not, as some modern Enlightenment thinkers would have us believe, the origin of religion and the sacred, but rather represent its most complete and absolute upheaval and distortion. The challenge is to be able to go back to an earlier phase, in which there is no trace of these sacrifices; but here the only thing historiography can tell us is that among peoples devoted to pastoralism or hunting these brutalities were absent.

BB: Farmer Cain sacrifices shepherd Abel.

AF: Exactly! However, it's a fact that true esotericism and the figures who appeared in the "axial period," such as Laozi, the "envoy of Heaven" (*tian ming*), helped to interrupt these practices.

BB: But don't the sinologists you mentioned, perhaps with the sole exception of the esotericist Matgioi, seem to agree that primitive Taoism was a form of shamanism?

AF: In fact, the historian is in a way professionally obliged to speak of this reality in terms of cultural categories, castes, hybridizations, borrowings, temporal succession. First this, then that, and so on. In short, the historical discipline always runs the risk of ignoring both synchronic and achronic, timeless, unclassifiable phenomena. Shamanism is seen as the antecedent of religion, or as a form of archaic, primitive religiosity. And then the most disparate elements are included: beliefs, religious practices, magic rituals, ecstatic, ethnomedical techniques, and so on. But thank God, not all shamans are the same! The shaman can be a sorcerer, a charlatan, but he can also be a seer, a mystic, a divine messenger, or, as the Taoists would say, a "true man" (*Tchenn-jen*). Certain forms of shamanism have merged with Taoism, and there has been, and still is, a shamanic Taoism; but always around a central core of original truths inspired, as I see it, from above or dictated by a form of celestial fulfillment or spiritual achievement that has nothing to do with what is normally understood by shamanism.

Taoist esotericism and politics

BB: Taoism has also often had a political significance. There have been Taoist-inspired popular revolts, and Taoism has even become a "state religion." What does this have to do with esotericism?

AF: I think at the root of these revolts was a real desire to re-establish—Taoist-style—a universal order. Incidentally, the *I Ching* and the *Tao te King* are also manuals of good governance. A totalizing, unitary vision of the cosmos cannot leave anything out, not even society, not even politics. The political implications—or as Silvano Panunzio would have said, metapolitical—are also to be found in Plato and Pythagoras. Now, on the relationship between politics and esotericism, which we cannot even briefly explain here, we refer you to the excellent journal *Politica Hermetica*, where you will find dense and enlightening scientific pages on this subject.

BB: According to your criteria of esotericism, would you say that primitive Taoism was elitist?

AF: Elitist, yes, in the sense that it was passed down from master to disciple.

The Dao way

BB: And what happened to the corresponding esoteric tradition?

AF: Formally, it was mainly transmitted in the *Tao Te King* or *Dao de jing* according to the established transliteration, the so-called *Book of Five Thousand Words*.

BB: What exactly do you mean by "*Dao*"?

AF: *Dao* means "Way," the "Way" according to which things become, or rather re-become, what they are. Basically, I think the comparison with Aristotle's "unmoved mover" may be acceptable insofar as the *Dao* moves everything but is moved by nothing, acts without being acted upon by anything and without acting in turn (the famous *wei-wu-wei*, "acting without acting"). In other words, it's an order immanent to things, an intrinsic quality, something that makes things be and is at the same time a way of being things.

BB: Are we in the realm of metaphysics or cosmology or both?

AF: Paradoxically—as you would probably say—the two domains here seem indissociable to me. Apparently, we start from nature and work our way back to God, or at least many of us might see it that way. However, I believe that our theological and philosophical categories are insufficient here, and that only a Taoist who follows his Way can truly understand its meaning. Above all, even when he has grasped it, he cannot explain it to us with the rigor we logicians would expect, for the secret of the *Dao* and the more remote "Great Dao" remains, in fact, inviolable. Inviolable because inexpressible. In fact, to preserve its qualities, the

Dao must remain hidden—or empty—and therefore must not be spoken of; but at the same time, it must be connected to, and therefore thought of, and in thinking it, it is spoken of in a certain way, which is why it ends up being given a name.

BB: Which symbol would best describe it?

AF: The Taoist canon is rich in images and symbols that explain the *Dao*. For example, air and water. The *Dao* is spread everywhere like the air—an image that can be associated with universality and transcendence—and at the same time is present in the breath of every human being—immanence. Similarly, water is capable of overcoming obstacles and adapting to all surfaces and containers—universality—but never loses its nature and integrity—immanence. The *Dao* is everything, and precisely because it is everything, is elusive. *Servata distantia*,[3] the Gospels remind us: "The wind blows where it wills, and you hear the sound of it; but you know not whence it comes, nor whither it goes. So it is with everyone who is born of the Spirit." (John 3:8)

Dao and Deus absconditus

BB: Do you see an analogy between the *Dao* and "our" *Deus absconditus*?

AF: We read it in the Old Testament: "*Vere tu es Deus absconditus*," "Truly you are a God that hides yourself." (Isa. 45:15) Of course, there is an analogy in the fact that we grasp the incommensurability and elusiveness of God, and therefore the impossibility for man to know him fully. It's a

---

[3] "Distance maintained," "all things considered."

concept that has been accepted by many Christian thinkers, from Nicolas of Cusa to Blaise Pascal. But I think that to find much more rigorous analogies, we need to refer to Heraclitus of Ephesus. Some researchers have hypothesized an analogy between the "unity of opposites" that emerges in Heraclitus' thought and the polarity typical of Chinese Taoism. Others have also found strong correspondences between his concept of *physis* as "spontaneous order" and the *Dao*.

BB: You refer to the action of the *Dao* through the mediation of the two opposing cosmic principles, *yin* (black) and *yang* (white)…

Yin and yang

AF: *Yin* and *Yang* had to do with the duality of night and day, or more precisely, the dark and sunny sides of mountains. These two principles are in fact at the root of many traditional Chinese sciences, from alchemy to traditional medicine, from martial arts to the *I Ching* itself. Obviously, we must distinguish between complementary cosmogonic principles and their reflection in existence. It's a conception that could be defined as polar or bipolar, bearing in mind that Taoists say that before the creation of the universe there is only *Wou-ki*, i.e., the "Apolar" or "Poleless." Then appeared what they call *Tai-ki*, the "Supreme Pole," which later divided into *Tien* (Heaven, essence) and *Ti* (Earth, substance). This polarization remains at the principial level, and it's only when the cosmos has manifested that we find the complementary cosmic principles *yin* and *yang*.

After all, I believe that this intuition means that the *Dao* is never given in absolute form, but always in the form of complementarity between opposites, and I'd like to say that the great secret of the *Dao* consists precisely in revealing to man that the nature of things is "relationship," "bond," "connection."

BB: It is these concepts that can be called "esoteric"…

AF: Indeed, this is a truth that is not a matter of thought or mere mental processes, but of knowledge of a higher order.

And here we find ourselves at the very heart of esotericism as a form of cosmic and metacosmic knowledge. It is by living in total symbiosis with nature and its rhythms that certain individuals endowed with special sensitivity and exceptional spiritual gifts manage to grasp the secrets of the cosmos. And then there are those who have the ability to translate this knowledge into symbols, images, words, and discursive wisdom. Whoever wrote the *Dao de jing* obviously possessed all these abilities.

Taoist esotericism and alchemy

BB: And what about Chinese alchemy?

AF: It's a very complex business (laughs). It is said that Chinese alchemy was interested in the quest for immortality, both through various elixirs and "magical" concoctions, and through complicated methods and techniques of endogenous transmutation of the body based on a precise knowledge of man's "occult physiology." Some believe these to be baseless speculations; others believe them to be true. As is often the case, the truth lies somewhere in between: on the one hand, Chinese alchemy used chemicals based on minerals, metals, and other natural substances, which often proved harmful, even fatal, to those who foolishly had the temerity to ingest them. On the other hand, precisely because of these failures, a highly refined *inner* alchemy developed, similar to that of Hindu yoga, based on techniques of meditation, dietetics, and physiological practices. We have a brilliant literary testimony to this in the treatise on *The Secret of the Golden Flower*.[4]

BB: To the best of my knowledge, this is the only known complete text on Chinese initiation practices.

AF: I can confirm this. To date, there is no other text as complete, accurate, and translated into a European language. It was the great sinologist Richard Wilhelm (1873–1930) who found it and translated it into German, and his friend Carl Gustav Jung who wrote his Commentary on the Mystery of the Golden Flower.[5]

Taoist esotericism and the quest for immortality

BB: Let's return to this quest for immortality, which seems to be a recurring theme in Chinese Taoism. What are its esoteric foundations?

AF: Well, I'd say the mysteries of death and the afterlife. Esotericism has always had a certain familiarity with death, with the "second death" and with "psychic death." Chinese esotericism is no exception. Taoists seek immortality, because they too want to conquer death. Of course, this aspiration has also given rise to recurrent misunderstandings and deviations, not only in popular Chinese culture, but also, it has to be said in all honesty, among a more cultivated and intellectually demanding public. And it is the latter who must be held primarily responsible for the circu-

[4] Lu Tsou (or Lu Yen), Tai Yi Kin Houa Tsoung Tchi (8th century).
[5] London: Kegan Paul, 1931.

lation of a false esoteric literature, which has done great harm to true Taoism.

BB: However, escaping physical decay and perhaps death is a very old idea, and not just a Chinese one.

AF: Indubitably! Traces of it can be found all the way from Asia to predynastic Egypt. If we think of the Christian conception of the "resurrection of the flesh," we don't stray far from this same idea. The resurrection of the flesh is an absolutely real fact for us, but there are those who interpret it in a materialistic sense. Something similar has happened, I think, with immortality in the Chinese tradition. In Taoism, physical immortality is understood in varying degrees.

BB: And what would be the highest rank?

AF: The ascent to Heaven in broad daylight. Taoist texts put it this way. The Taoist who has attained the highest degree of spiritual realization becomes capable of passing his entire body into the invisible, without leaving a trace. Even Chinese historical documents attest to this, or so sinologists tell us. These apotheoses are said to have taken place in the presence of hundreds of witnesses. Of course, we can't know if this is true, but I suspect it could be. On the other hand, our Bible also speaks of similar cases, see Enoch and Elijah, not forgetting the Assumption of the Virgin Mary.

BB: After all, even some Indian and Tibetan yoga practices were, and still are, aimed at this same goal.

AF: Yes, of course. And on the other hand, you have to take into consideration the fact that Chinese Taoism has hybridized in various ways, notably with Buddhism, but above all with Tibetan Tantrism.

Taoism: an esotericism

BB: So, do you see Taoism as pure esotericism and Laozi as a "father" of esotericism?

AF: Yes. The original impulse of Taoism is intimately esoteric. In the beginning, the relationship between adept and master and between adept and "spiritual powers" was fundamental. Hierarchical order, doctrine, and relative rites came later, as did the "Taoist religion" in its institutional form. Laotzi, or someone on his behalf, wrote down the teachings, and in this sense can be considered the "father" of a "school." But then, we must remember that Chinese is an ideographic and symbolic script, very difficult to render in discursive thought. I have five versions of the *Dao de jing*, and they're all very different from one another. This is why I believe that Taoism is almost inaccessible to most of us, and that some of its doctrines can only be approached—and I won't say understood—from an esoteric point of view, i.e., *ab intra*, by identification.

BB: To conclude, what would you say is the chief aim of Taoism from an esoteric point of view?

AF: To be in perfect harmony with the world, in peace of heart and, in short, in original simplicity. As far as I'm concerned, Laozi could also have been illiterate (and perhaps he really was) and his actual teaching "mute." What is certain is that his "experience" is no different from that of the Buddha or that of all those who belong to what I like to call "the golden chain." The synergetic syncretism that has developed between Taoism and certain "foreign" traditions is a masterly testimony to this. In fact, truth may take many names and many forms, but in essence it remains unique. Knowing how to grasp this fundamental unity, not only intellectually but also, as our medieval scholastics would have said, *sub specie interioritatis* (from the perspective of interiority), means becoming part of it, and being able to bear witness to it in the world, as the great Laotzi did with incomparable mastery.

Chapter 14
Modern Esotericism

The paroxysm of esotericism and occultism in the 19ᵗʰ century, followed by the codification of esotericism by René Guénon, has not stopped the emergence of modern esotericism, even if it was a resurgence of older esotericism (Rosicrucianism, for example). The purpose of this interview is to discuss the relevance of modern esotericism.

BB: Are the *New Age*, certain personal developments, and ufology really modern esotericism? Do these currents of thought have more or less to do with traditional esotericism?

AF: In our previous interview, we talked about Taoism and recalled the existence of a "popular Taoism," i.e., an esotericism open to all. At first glance, as the Latins would say, this would be a *contradictio in adjecto*.[1] Indeed, how can a domain reserved for the privileged few enter the public sphere? The truth is, these two domains have nothing to do with each other. What the public hears about is nothing more than the outer wrapping of esotericism, and what's more, in degraded or counterfeit forms; and this at the theoretical level. On the "practical" level, things are no better, for then it's the "powers" and "phenomena" that are given importance, rather than the spiritual realities that underlie them.

---

[1] Literally: "contradiction in terms."

BB: Not to mention imagination and curiosity, which make the whole thing even worse.

Nineteenth-century occultism and contemporary New Age

AF: Exactly. This applies to the *New Age*, but one could say it also applies to the occultism of the 19ᵗʰ and 20ᵗʰ centuries.

BB: Having said that, when we talk about the *New Age*, we're mostly referring to the Anglo-American world and the *underground* culture of the '60s, whereas European occultism was a less ideological and perhaps more "dressed up" phenomenon. What are the differences between these "movements"?

AF: In both cases, on a social level, they were "reactions." Reaction to mass culture in the case of *New Age*, reaction to positivism and scientism in the case of European occultism. And here I'd like to say, adopting a symbolism familiar to the Western esoteric tradition, that it's always the "law of equilibrium" which governs certain processes: when a force is applied to the end of a lever, a rotational movement is determined which is stopped by an equal and opposite force acting on the other end. We speak of a banal "social mechanism," but this compensating or regulating mechanism, if we prefer, acts in all spheres of existence and seems to have a cosmic character.

BB: So, in terms of modern age esotericism, is it too much to speak of "cultural fashions"?

AF: I mean it, when "fashion" designates a simple pattern of behavior that asserts itself on a collective and social level. In fact, we're not talking here about simple behavior patterns, but about individual and collective processes in which extra-individual and extra-subjective forces are at work. What's at work is a "law of compensation," which even Jung intuited—except that he explained it using the idea of the individual and collective unconscious.

BB: Would you say there's an unconscious tendency to balance?

AF: Precisely. And then the interest itself in the "esoterological" tendency would be nothing more than a psychogenic symptom deriving from a lack of congruence between the conscious and the unconscious, a congruence that should exist in the normal state. But in my opinion there's much more to it than that; there's a primal "need" inherent in man and claiming its rights. I'm talking about fundamental needs, in this case the spiritual need; so it's the soul itself, and not just the psyche, that clamors, and even clamors imperatively. It's a hunger that must be satisfied in one way or another. And when you're hungry, you'll jump at anything, even spoiled, adulterated, or counterfeit food.

BB: Would you say that neo-spiritualism is comparable to counterfeit food?

AF: Absolutely! But you understand that it's always better to eat something than to die of hunger. However, the important thing is to know this, to be aware of it, and then try to remedy it by seeking out better, healthier, and more nutritious foods. The reasoning we follow here should also serve this purpose.

BB: I couldn't agree more! Returning to contemporary pseudo-esotericism, what are the elements that distance it from true esotericism?

Pseudo-esotericisms and religion

AF: Well, from my point of view, I'd say first and foremost hostility towards "traditional religions," which sometimes even translates into hostility towards the institutions themselves. I'm thinking in particular of the hatred of the Catholic religion, fueled in the past by Gnostic groups, by "magical," pseudo-hermetic or neopagan brotherhoods, but also by deviant fringes of Freemasonry. Some of today's alleged "esoterists"—heirs to an adulterated bookish scholasticism—talk a lot about spiritual tolerance, but when you talk to them about the Church, all they see are bonfires and inquisitions. That they see nothing else seems to me frankly a little strange and suspicious. There is no fairness, balance, or wisdom in such a harsh judgment.

BB: Don't these attitudes belong more to sects than to "esotericism" *per se*?

AF: The problem is that today it's hard to tell the difference between a religious sect and an esoteric brotherhood. They look the same, and even the reasoning behind them has a lot in common. I don't want to generalize, but most of the time I've found this to be the case. So we can't complain if sociologists get a little confused in cataloguing and classifying these phenomena.

BB: You spoke of hostility towards institutions. What "esoteric" realities are you referring to in particular?

AF: I'm thinking of the links between certain brotherhoods and subversive movements and even terrorism. Some time ago, a book was published in Italy entitled *Esoterismo e politica occulta: dai templari alle Brigate rosse* [Esoterism and Occult Politics. From the Knights Templar to the Red Brigades] (Taranto: Dellisanti, 2005). In it, Romeo Frigiola supports the thesis of such links. Of course, the matter is highly complex, and there would be countless clarifications and distinctions to be made for a precise historical reconstruction of these interferences, which I would define as "crypto-political" rather than political; but whatever the case, the link between certain ideas conveyed by pseudo-esoteric circles and certain disastrous ideologies that have infested the world over the last three or four centuries is certainly an indisputable fact.

BB: For example?

AF: Jean Guitton (1901–1999), an authoritative Catholic philosopher of the last century, has argued for the continuity of the old dualistic pseudo-gnosis in contemporary thought. All rigidly opposed conceptions not only have a disruptive effect on people's psychic equilibrium, but can also induce criminal behavior. Similarly, ascribing intentions to Nature, conceiving her as a demiurgic or even an evil stepmother—another absurdity of Gnostic ideation—obliterates forever the possibility of wonder and contemplation, and can justify carelessness and even violence towards her. I'm obviously not saying that these ideas come directly from false esotericism, but I am saying that false esotericism has created the ideological presuppositions and the corresponding mental attitudes that help to distance one from an upright and correct vision of things.

Gnosis or Gnosticism?

BB: This is the difference between true gnosis and what has rightly been called "gnosticism."

AF: Precisely! This point cannot be stressed enough. Gnosis is the realization of a spiritual state, while Gnosticism is a twisting and turning of thought upon itself. Gnosis and gnosticism are diametrically opposed.

BB: Would you associate the doctrines of modern "esotericism" with "gnosticism"?

AF: I'd say most of them are, but in the sense that they're mystifications, falsifications, adulterations, and counterfeits of genuine esoteric doctrines. Think, for example, of all that has been said and written about so-called "reincarnation"—one of the fundamental dogmas of pseudo-esotericism—compared with what Hindu doctrines have actually written and said on the subject.

BB: I'd like to clarify: do you see contemporary false esotericism, or, if you prefer, that of the last three centuries, as related to true esotericism or to ancient false esotericism?

AF: In my opinion, there is no real continuity, not even with the false esotericism of antiquity. Man and his environment have changed so much that links with the past seem irretrievably broken. We don't really know how the people of the Middle Ages and the Renaissance felt and thought. However, certain ideas, teachings, and knowledge were indeed passed on without interruption. But sometimes those who received them didn't really understand them. Of course, there are exceptions, and I think René Guénon is one of them.

BB: René Guénon remains an enigma. Do you see him as a "scholastic" and, perhaps, as a student of esotericism?

AF: Yes, of course. In a way, we owe everything we can say about esotericism to him. With his astonishing intelligence and great sensitivity, he was able to say the right things.

There was no one in the 20th century who equaled him—not even today. He is a milestone, an "Aquinas" of esotericism, so to speak. After all, even those who have criticized or denigrated him owe him everything. So, let's be clear, we don't need to make him a saint, but only to benefit from his indications and teachings, of course with discernment.

BB: Coming back to pseudo-esotericism, is there a link with the deviated esotericism of the past or are they two different manifestations?

Some contemporary esoteric falsehoods

AF: There is certainly an indirect link. I don't know if a continuity can be demonstrated, but no doubt there is no lack of analogies between these two realities. Jesus accused the rulers of Israel—the esoteric sect of the Pharisees—of withholding from the people the correct "keys" to reading the Holy Scriptures and, today, these keys are apparently offered to everyone instead. But the truth is that these "keys" don't open any doors, and we've gone from an occultation that wanted to hide the truth as much as possible for reasons of power, to revelations of distorted, denatured, deformed truths.

BB: And the "secrets"? It seems that certain organizations that allege links with authentic esoteric lines of descent from the past are preserving who knows what disturbing and terrible truths. What do you think they are?

AF: Usually, these secrets have more to do with practical, operational, or ritual aspects… than with unspoken mysteries. At the very least, they may involve contents that are difficult to understand, or "codes" that only an initiate can decipher and make the object of meditation. In some cases, these contents are locked away in ancient texts, preserved and handed down for generations. Secrets can also include obscene sexual practices totally invented from Indian tantra practices, i.e., essentially perverted. But as Guénon reminded us, the real "initiatory secret" is simply the inexpressible, incommunicable part of a higher, transcendent truth. Everything else is raw material, reserved for initiates, or rather "students" under the guidance of a master.

BB: Speaking of "confidential content," it does seem that something of it leaks out from time to time.

AF: More than just something. In the late 1980s, for example, a Milanese group called "Prometheus," led by former *Red Brigade* member Paolo Fogagnolo, published texts documenting a type of alchemical operation practiced by the Egyptian Osirian Order: the selective inner circle of the Mystical and Therapeutic Brotherhood of the Myriam, founded by Giuliano Kremmerz. These were "Osirian" operative practices aimed at creating a "body of light" or "immortal body of glory." I myself came into possession of these documents for study purposes and eventually, as already stated, realized that, taken out of context, they were completely useless materials. Another book containing many indiscretions about pseudo-esoteric groups was Massimo Introvigne's famous essay *Il cappello del mago* [The magician's hat].[2]

BB: And what about ufology? Has it played a role in the pseudo-esotericism of the modern era?

AF: Certainly, and that's always the case. However, I would

[2] *Il cappello del mago. I nuovi movimenti magici dallo spiritismo al satanismo* (Milan: SugarCo, 1990).

like to make it clear that UFOS (unidentified flying objects) are one thing, and the many far-fetched theories about them another. UFOs are an absolutely real phenomenon and worthy of study. The extraterrestrial theme generally associated with them long predates the phenomenon as we know it, and has sometimes crept into theories of pseudo-esotericism.

BB: You're referring to "The Coming Race" imagined by Bulwer Lytton and the Lam entity conjured up by A. Crowley.[3]

AF: Not only that. I'm also referring to "contactism," which has many links with pseudo-esoteric organizations and the cult of flying saucers or, as Jean Robin has defined it, "discosophical cultism." Among these unspoken secrets reserved for small circles of "initiates" was precisely that of the extraterrestrial origin of the human race and the presence of these entities in human history since the foundation of the world. Today the subject is discussed with greater ease even within Masonic lodges. These are the *Unknown Superiors*, whom many occultists consider to be the inspirers and guardians of initiation and esoteric Tradition. René Guénon has also dealt with these *Unknown Superiors*, but it's clear that for him the question must be considered from a purely symbolic point of view; extraterrestrials have nothing to do with it.

---

[3] "Lam's Portrait" is the sketch of a being with a huge skull, presented at the "Dead Souls" exhibition organized by Aleister Crowley in Greenwich Village, New York, in 1919, then inserted as a frontispiece in his magazine *The Equinox*, vol. III, no. I, Spring 1919 (Detroit, MI: Universal Publishing Co), with the indication: "LAM is the Tibetan word for Way or Path, and LAMA is He who goeth…"

BB: There is a book by Louis de Maistre on this subject, *L'énigme René Guénon et les supérieurs inconnus. Contribution à l'étude de l'histoire mondiale "souterraine"* (Milan: Arché, 2009).

AF: It's undoubtedly an interesting book, which takes stock of the complex question from a historical point of view, but we're in the realm of conspiracy. Guénon, on the other hand, always pointed out that such a question could neither be tackled nor resolved by historians. The question is whether there are individuals who have reached the highest peaks of spiritual realization, perhaps endowed with longevity or even immortality, such as the Wandering Jew or the Prophet Elijah, St John, "the disciple who will never die," or the Count de Saint-Germain or Fulcanelli. Guénon in *The King of the World*, quoting Ibn 'Arabi, speaks of a "hierarchy of saints" and "world guardians."[4] Basically, it's not a very different idea from what we Christians call *communio sanctorum* (the communion of saints).

BB: The communion of saints is to "unknown superiors" what truth is to fiction, is it not?

AF: Exactly! In other words, spiritual truth is becoming secularized. Guénon has, in my opinion, contributed to restoring a sacred and spiritual connotation to the idea of "unknown superiors," whereas occultists have lent it a completely legendary and imaginative connotation—cosmologized at the very least.

BB: Should the process of secularization be seen as involving both the religious sphere and esotericism?

[4] Ibn 'Arabi, *Il mistero dei custodi del mondo* [The mystery of the guardians of the world] (Ed. Il Leone Verde, 2001).

AF: I'd say that it's not esotericism itself that's becoming secularized, just as it's not religion itself that's becoming secularized. Truth can be grasped at any time by anyone who places themselves in the right conditions to receive it. What changes is the interpretation of truth, its cultural and social translation. It's the world that becomes fiction, swallowing up and phagocytizing everything in that fiction, even the most sacred and inviolable.

BB: This is what Nietzsche says in *Twilight of the Idols*: "I'm going to explain to you how the real world ended up becoming a fairy tale." But when and where does this process of moving away from its core of intangible truths towards esotericism begin?

AF: Probably from the invention of writing. The "scribal" dimension certainly facilitated this rejection of the truth, above all because it rendered orality and therefore the figure of the Master useless. The deviations all stemmed from a misleading interpretation of ancient doctrines and teachings, borrowed or even challenged by those no longer capable of understanding them.

BB: You could say that the theoretical-speculative dimension is taking precedence over the mystical and initiatory dimension of esotericism...

AF: Yes, something like that. This is also mentioned in reference to the transition from operative to speculative Freemasonry, but it's a transition that has affected more or less all the "initiatory organizations" of the past. When certain truths are put down in writing, it's not uncommon for them to be misunderstood and thus distorted.

BB: We read it in the Gospel: "Do not give the holy things to the dogs, and do not cast your pearls before swine, lest they trample them under their feet and turn and tear you to pieces." (Matt. 7:6) But then, is this the fate of esotericism?

Esotericism and counterfeits

AF: Let's say it's the destiny of everything that enters the sphere of this world transformed and made more complex by a certain human type that has come to predominate from a certain period onwards. On the other hand, even religions are well aware of these processes of decadence, stiffening, and dissolution. The sun rises and sets, the moon has its phases too: waxing and waning, full moon, and new moon, first quarter and last quarter. In my opinion, the metaphor of the moon's phases can help us understand the deeper reasons behind these anthropological and social changes. And it's a "rule" that also applies to the outer forms of esotericism; but, I repeat, an essential core of truth is always present and available to those capable of understanding it.

BB: What would be the major criterion for distinguishing genuine esotericism from its counterfeits?

AF: In fact, there is one, and it's very simple. Esotericism, as we've said, always presupposes a "golden chain" of masters who pass on the baton. A master is not the one who can teach something—in other words, a mere instructor—but the one who knows how to transmit mastery and turn the student into a new master.

BB: In modern esoteric "movements," does this transmission still take place from master to disciple, from mouth to ear?

Transmissions and discontinuities

AF: I think that within some very small organizations, and not known to the public, something like this still happens. Certainly not in those associative structures that are open to all and run membership campaigns!

BB: Are there any that can be named here?

AF: Of all the organizations that can be described as "esoteric," a certain Freemasonry certainly still has its intrinsic validity in terms of initiation, ritual, and richness of symbolism. I wouldn't say the same of any other known organization. However, for a devout Catholic, the problem with such dual membership remains, and I frankly advise against it. At least until the Church decides otherwise, which I doubt very much for many reasons we can't go into here.

BB: Would you say that the principle of "historical continuity" is still valid, in the absence of which there would be no true esotericism?

AF: I think that certain temporal fractures and discontinuities surely had an impact. When a tradition is interrupted, it cannot be artificially reconstructed piece by piece. But it is always possible that an exceptional and particularly gifted personality will manage, by "the will of Heaven," to restore what has been interrupted, and to resume, so to speak, "the thread of the conversation." This is a possibility, just as there is the possibility of a "family" line of succession and transmission. But I don't think we can say anything definitive and certain about these possibilities, for which there are also important traces and studies.

BB: Has there been any "updating" of what has been defined as "traditional esotericism," or any resurgence of esoteric currents closely linked to the context of a traditional religion?

AF: Rather than actualizations or resurgences, I would speak of "intellectual currents" that have fulfilled a function analogous to that once performed externally by certain "philosophical schools," themselves emanations of genuine esoteric organizations of their own. I'm thinking, for example, of the "traditional" thought inaugurated by René Guénon. This thinking has succeeded in spreading in many directions and germinating spiritual currents within religions themselves.

BB: This influence has not always been positive!

AF: Indeed, when it stimulated a "return to Tradition," in a spiritual sense or in the sense of valorizing the *depositum fidei* of different traditions, it was positive; when, on the contrary, it produced abjurations, it was negative. But it has to be said in all honesty that the responsibility for these abjurations lies with the misunderstandings of certain readers, and not with the message itself, which never suggested or solicited them. So, of course, there are many writers who draw their inspiration from this current, but not all of them have such clear ideas as did René Guénon.

BB: Which authors, would you say, were ideally linked to Guénon and acted within their respective traditions in the direction of esotericism?

Religious esotericism

AF: For Christianity, we could mention Abbé Henri Stéphane (1907–1985), to whom François Chenique (1927–2012) and Jean Borella (1930–) were linked. In Italy, two authors of reference for Christian esotericism were Paolo

Marchetti Virio and Silvano Panunzio whom I've already mentioned. But the names are numerous, and we can speak of a veritable "school of Christian esotericism," which continues to have valuable representatives even today. As for Islam, I'm thinking of the many leading scholars of Islamic studies who have drawn attention to esoteric schools, such as Louis Massignon (1883–1962), Henry Corbin (1903–1978) and René Guénon himself (1886–1951); for Judaism, the authors of reference are those who have focused on the Kabbalah, such as Leo Schaya (1916–1985), Gershom Scholem (1897–1982) and today Moshe Idel (1947–); for Hinduism: Ananda Kentish Coomaraswamy (1877–1947) and Alain Daniélou (1907–1944); for Buddhism: Marco Pallis (1895–1989), Jean Marquès-Rivière (1903–2000), and Alexandra David-Néel (1868–1969); for Taoism: Eugène Albert Puyou de Pouvourville (1861–1939) alias Matgioi; and for Tantrism: Sir John Woodroffe (1865–1936), also known by the pseudonym Arthur Avalon.

BB: There's so much more to say about each of these illustrious names, but this interview is coming to an end. In conclusion, I understand that despite the cultural revival and "religious awakening" that these currents have brought about, and for which they must certainly be appreciated, in the West there are very few genuine esoteric traditions left?

AF: That's right! even if we talk about it a lot, as we are doing in these interviews. We can only hope that it's not just about talking about it! (laughs).

Chapter 15
Esotericism and Metaphysics

Esotericism regularly involves metaphysics. Yet these two approaches are quite distinct. The purpose of this interview is to clarify their respective approaches and points of view.

BB: Metaphysics was used, notably by Guénon in his codification of esotericism, confirming, if proof were needed, his role as a *line judge* in the field. However, some esotericism incorporates metaphysics. How would you characterize the difference between the two approaches?

AF: To simplify, I'd say that metaphysics is the fullness of Truth, and therefore the end, while esotericism is a path by which it is possible to reach it.

Pure intellect and creative imagination

BB: But, when we talk about metaphysical doctrines, aren't we also talking about a body of knowledge or principles organically elaborated by someone? Isn't there also a "theory" behind every metaphysical doctrine?

AF: For Plato Θεωρία (*theoria*) is "the contemplation of the totality of time and being." In this sense we could also say that metaphysics is pure theory, but the organ best suited to it is certainly not reason or discursive thought, it's the spiritual intellect or pure intellect. Guénon was also convinced of this, and equated it with Hindu *vidya* or supreme knowledge.

BB: In fact, as Plato made clear: "Theoretical discourse is the last resort in the teaching of truth."[1] So, if the pure intellect is the organ of metaphysics, what organ is best suited for esotericism?

AF: I would say, in agreement with Corbin, "creative imagination." "Creative," as the great Islamic scholar explains,[2] means feeding the infinite spaces of the spiritual imagination with vital, fertile impulses. In this sense, it's as if the esotericist assumes a divine quality, that of "creative power," so to speak. But we must not confuse the imaginative with the imaginary, a confusion into which false esotericism often falls. Such esotericism is then no more than the fruit of fantasies and produces only false illusions. The illusion of possessing the truth is generally a very dangerous and harmful thing, both mentally and spiritually.

BB: And what relationship do you see between creative imagination and pure intellect?

AF: I would say that the imaginal faculty is a reflection of the pure intellect on the mental plane. But with the imagination we're in the realm of mental faculties, undoubtedly superior to thought but closely linked to it. This is why esotericism speaks of "purification of the mind," which is the aim of all meditating and, above all, concentrating activities. A purified mind is capable of "dialoguing" with the pure intellect in much the same way as, if you'll forgive the parallel, a man of faith dialogues with his guardian angel. In both cases, we're talking about a "heavenly inter-

---

[1] *Letter VII*, 326a–b.
[2] Henry Corbin, *Creative Imagination in the Sufism of Ibn 'Arabi* (Princeton, NJ: Princeton University Press, 1981).

mediary," i.e., the *interiore homine* expression of a divine attribute.

BB: Would you say that the more the soul is transparent and permeable to divine light, the more the imagination will conform to it, developing creative capacities in imitation of God?

AF: I'd say so. It is by virtue of the creative power of its intellect that the soul sees and perceives internally. Of course, you never can be sure that you're saying things right, because you first have to be aware of the limitations of human language. Logic and precision must never be lacking, even when dealing with the most elevated questions, but always with the awareness that these are only stammerings and approximations of the truth. A Catholic theologian, for example, might object to all that has been said so far, on the grounds that without fidelity to the Magisterium there can be no true theology. That's why our interviews are not intended to be a theological discourse, but rather to share the reflections of two laymen on a subject that is certainly difficult and controversial, but worthy of being approached honestly and above all without prejudice.

BB: *Excusatio non petita, accusatio manifesta!*[3]

AF: (Laughs). You're right; I wish I'd said that at the beginning of our talks, certainly not to justify myself, but to make people aware that Christians shouldn't be afraid to express their ideas, even when they don't strictly conform to current orthodoxy. And this especially when they are not

---

[3] The literal translation of this Latin proverb of medieval origin is "unsolicited apology, manifests accusation"; an equivalent form is "whoever excuses himself accuses himself."

so, for we should never weary of providing useful stimuli to deepen our knowledge of the things that really matter and that are or should be important for those to whom the keys to the Kingdom have been entrusted by divine mandate.[4]

Esotericism and cosmology

BB: This joke, this provocation will at least have clarified things! Let's get back to the relationship between metaphysics and esotericism, or, it could just as well be said, between metaphysics and cosmology, for, with esotericism, we remain in the sphere of manifestation, whereas with metaphysics we're in a sphere that goes beyond it.

AF: Yes, provided we make it clear right away that by cosmos we don't mean the nature or environment that shelters the Earth as a planet, but a vaster reality that includes the visible and the invisible. In short, we're talking about an "inner" Cosmos, a Cosmos of the Soul reflected in the outer Cosmos. Esotericism has nothing to do with science, nor is it, as some misleading interpretations would have us believe, "another science," analogous in this sense to so-called parapsychology, with which it is now often confused or even replaced. With metaphysics, on the contrary, it is indeed a celestial supra-cosmos, but one that is also in some way "interior."

BB: And isn't this then a realm that even the creative imagination cannot reach?

---

[4] "Because he [Peter] has received the keys of the kingdom of heaven, the power to bind and loose is entrusted to him; the care of the whole Church and its government are given to him" [*cura ei totius Ecclesiae et principatus committitur*]; Pope Gregory I, Epist. lib. V, ep. xx, in P.L. LXXVII, 745.

AF: It's true! The Cosmos is a kind of springboard for the Soul, as the "Tomb of the Diver" at Paestum aptly illustrates. Having reached its maximum effort, the Soul with its imaginative and creative faculty (Dante would speak of "high fantasy,"[5] but it's the same thing), must plunge into the depths of divine mystery or eternity.

Esotericism and symbolism

BB: So, in what sense can the esotericist participate in this unspeakably "sublime experience," or, as you put it, prepare the way for it?

AF: Through the Symbol, the Symbol as apparition and epiphany of spiritual Truth! Esotericism as I understand it, that is, from my point of view, is nothing other than an acted symbol, a *mysterium*, a "secret that is acted and displayed"[6] (I'm using Jung's expressions, but in no way espousing his point of view). The esotericist is the one who manages to see the cosmic symbolism latent in all things, and to experience it. And if the experience is true and sincere, it is inevitable that it will lead him to the One who is the Lord of all things, the metacosmic origin of the whole universe.

BB: Is it a mystical experience in the full sense of the word, or a purely "intuitive" one?

AF: Good question! I think both are possible. The two "results" are not mutually exclusive, provided the seeker-initiate has followed the right path, without getting lost in the complex labyrinth of his mind. Let me remind you of

[5] *Divine Comedy*, Paradise, Canto XXXIII, v. 145.
[6] *Psychology and Religion: West and East*, vol. 11, 2nd ed. (Princeton, NJ: Princeton University Press, 1969), 379.

the experience of French occultist Paul Sédir[7] who succeeded in making the leap from a false esotericism (the Martinist Order) to a kind of "pure evangelism."

BB: An exception to the rule...

AF: No doubt, but it's an example of how, if you have the right spirit and are honest to the core, you can achieve the highest spiritual goal.

BB: And what would be the classic passage made by a pure esotericist? Can we mention at least one name?

AF: It's the passage from polarity to unity, from duality to identity. It's difficult to name names, as the true esotericists are anonymous and their names are generally heteronomous. We've spoken of the greatest as the "fathers of esotericism"; I think their examples and testimonies are more than sufficient.

Metaphysics and esotericism: the passage through "death"

BB: If I'm not mistaken, I understand that the true esotericists, according to you, were also authoritative "metaphysicians"?

AF: You're a great interpreter! (laughs). I'll say it without further ado: you don't enter metaphysics without first having passed through the place of death, without first having faced a real "journey into Hades." Dante, who, in my opinion, was one of the greatest esotericists in known history, amply demonstrated and explained this in his extraordinary popular work. But there's also Homer, and I would add Virgil, equally great and important figures whom I would

---

[7] Paul Sédir (born Yvon Le Loup), 1871–1926.

undoubtedly rank among the representatives of the most authentic "esotericism."

BB: So, as you've already pointed out, true esotericism is that which puts the individual in a position to "die to himself." Is that it?

AF: Yes, absolutely. Esotericism is to katabasis (Greek καταβάσις, "descent," from κατα "down" and βαίνω, "I'm going") what metaphysics is to anabasis (Greek ἀνάβασις, literally "going up").

BB: Perhaps it's because of this necessary "descent into hell" that esotericism has undergone major deviations.

AF: One might legitimately think so, but I don't believe that René Guénon's definition of "counter-initiation" elucidates precisely this possibility of inversion. In such a "descent," one can also lose oneself and become attached, so to speak, to the world below, with all the consequences for the Soul that one can only imagine.

Esoteric path and metaphysical safeguard

BB: Wouldn't a metaphysical perspective help to avoid such a result?

AF: I think so. Knowing where you're going to land right from the start, and realizing right away that you'll be dealing with superhuman forces, could be a good antidote to some of the poisons to which esotericism somehow exposes the initiate. To avoid global catastrophe, you need a global vision. Your books (all of them), and I'm not saying this out of flattery, represent a formidable and perhaps truly unique tool in the world panorama of traditional studies.

BB: You're too kind, but let's stay focused on this interview. For all we've said so far, esotericism is also "total knowledge" or rather Wisdom, as Panunzio would have said. What is metaphysics in relation to this knowledge-wisdom?

AF: Metaphysics is the essential, impassable limit or, as the Latins would say, the *non plus ultra*, the extreme limit that can be reached and beyond which it is impossible to go. It's important to set this limit, even on a rational level, because everything human is finite and limited. Man alone cannot go beyond himself. Hence the exhortation "know thyself" (ancient Greek γνῶθι σαυτόν, *gnothi sauton*, or γνῶθι σεαυτόν, *gnothi seauton*) from the temple of Apollo at Delphi. A knowledge of the Beyond would be in fact an entirely spiritual "non-knowledge" or "mystical knowledge" that can only be attained after an "initiatory death." Unless the seed falls and is buried, it cannot bear fruit.

BB: Would you say that the Greek maxim is therefore a synthesis of what true esotericism should aspire to?

AF: Yes, I really think so. But it's a gnosis preparatory to real gnosis, which is metaphysical in nature, far beyond the limits of the human intellect. True gnosis is divine, and this is what metaphysics reminds esotericism of. The unmistakable proof of divinity requires that God be conceived as living in a corporeal human existence. But here we enter into the "mysteries" of Christianity, which go beyond the present discussion.

BB: Can we sum up what you've explained by saying that the esoteric dimension doesn't access the metacosm—the realm of metaphysics—and that it can deviate into the infracosm?

AF: Yes, I think you could put it that way, with one caveat: when the esotericist deviates, the responsibility is "personal" and not attributable to esotericism itself. Some esoteric ideas, if misunderstood, can worsen the individual's situation rather than promote spiritual growth. So when I speak of "bogus esotericism," I'm referring precisely to certain "misunderstandings" due to the inability of certain individuals to understand the true meaning of "esoteric doctrines." The problem is that these individuals then become the leaders of pseudo-spiritual and pseudo-religious sects and associations that end up casting a negative shadow over the whole context.

BB: Would you say that this disadvantage, on the other hand, would not exist in metaphysics?

AF: Yes and no, because even in the field of metaphysics we can talk of misunderstandings of varying depths. For example, when metaphysics is reduced to a mere branch of philosophy, and a simple rational discourse is made of it to the detriment of its intrinsically spiritual dimension.

BB: It's true, just as Plato said.[8] It's also true when metaphysics is posited, beyond all religion, as the *religio perennis*, universal metaphysics and "absolute esotericism," turning revealed religions into "saving mirages" (in the words of Frithjof Schuon).[9]

Since metaphysics, even universal metaphysics, is in no way a religion, what would you say is the object or purpose of metaphysics?

---

[8] Cf. page 172.

[9] *Form and Substance in the Religions*, trans. M. Perry & J.-P. LaFouge (Bloomington, IN: World Wisdom, 2002), 145.

Esotericism and metaphysics: how they complement each other

AF: To make it clear that spiritual reality operates beyond any speculative thought. But not in the sense of a separate existence, but in the sense of an existence that is found in the Principle that generated it and from which it springs eternally. Metaphysics as a "total science" must lead man to find himself in God, at the highest and most elevated point possible, beyond the Cosmos. The task of esotericism is thus to prepare the mind to open up to transcendence.

BB: So you see esotericism and metaphysics as complementary.

AF: Yes, indeed. I don't think they're separable, they're part of the same circuit and travel in the same direction.

BB: Isn't it then difficult to integrate such a vision into the Christian perspective as proposed by the ecclesiastical Magisterium?

AF: I realize that, but I don't want to dwell on it here. The truth of the Gospel is beyond the scope of this discussion. Suffice it to say here that the goal of authentic esotericism and true metaphysics, whatever their "outer forms" and whatever their corresponding doctrines, is absolute purity, absolute perfection, and absolute holiness.

BB: Certainly, but do you think then that it is humanly possible to pursue such lofty ends; and don't such ends discourage even the most daring souls?

AF: It's not important that such a goal is actually attainable, but it is fundamental that it appears and can be contemplated, even from a distance. The highest mountain on our planet, Everest at 8,848 meters, seemed inaccessible, but Edmund Hillary and Sherpa Tenzing Norgay were incredibly successful. I mean, you can't cut down mountains just to prevent someone from trying to reach their summit sooner or later. Let's leave the landscape intact and avoid tampering with it! Even the "landscape of the spirit," if you'll pardon the metaphor, demands this absolute form of respect. The more beautiful, untouched, and vast it is, the more man will feel drawn to it and eager to travel far and wide.

BB: In short, it's all about placing man in front of the infinite.

AF: Exactly! He will acquire not only the ability to see and think big, but also the capacity to contemplate, with the requisite intensity and awe, the boundless beauty and depths of spiritual realities here and beyond.

Chapter 16

Esotericism and "Cognitive Humility"

Carlo Gambescia has spoken of "cognitive humility" with regard to esotericism. Insofar as esotericism proposes knowledge, what about such knowledge, and what's the best attitude to adopt towards it? This is the theme of this interview.

BB: Carlo Gambescia mentioned your "cognitive humility,"[1] precisely in the context of reading and reviewing esoteric works. How do you maintain such an attitude when you have privileged access to knowledge, and why?

AF: Thank you for this question, which gives me the opportunity to clarify my real position on esotericism. Of course, I don't want to personalize the discourse too much, even though I'm perfectly aware that in relation to everything we've said so far, this is just my opinion. It should be quite clear that, on this issue, there are very different points of view and even irreconcilable positions.

Truth and opinions

BB: What do you think is behind this irreconcilability and diversity of opinion?

AF: This obviously depends on the diversity with which

---

[1] In https://cargambesciametapolitics.altervista.org/lumilta-cognitiva
-di-aldo-la-fata/.

human beings relate to things, but also on the wide variety of angles and speculative perspectives. We will find this lack of consensus and agreement in all sectors of human knowledge, and it will be necessary for man to reconcile himself to it.

Heraclitus in his fragment 53, says: "War is the mother of all things, the queen of all things, and it makes some appear as gods, others as men, and it makes some free, and others slaves." *Polemos* (war) in Greek can also be translated as "contention," equivalent to polemic, discussion, dispute, contestation. In other words, all human relationships are governed by an irreducible diversity of opinions. There are those who manage to take advantage of this and those who don't, because in the end, what counts is not the right or wrong opinions, but what these opinions do to the men who hold them. It's the anthropological and human results that count, not the ideas themselves.

BB: But aren't we then inclined to posit a relativism of ideas?

AF: Yes, but only on a certain level. In fact, I'm not saying that all ideas are equal, and I'm not denying that there are erroneous, false, or imprecise opinions or, on the contrary, correct, exact, and precise ideas. What I'm saying is that we need to take note of the sophism intrinsic to all ideas, of the error present in every one of them, even in those that seem most in line with the truth.

BB: In Buddhism, there's a maxim that opinion is far removed from the perfect, and that "opinion" only becomes "vision" in the perfect.

AF: This is a criterion of truth that can certainly be shared. Truth only begins to appear when man learns to see things from above or, as Spinoza suggested, *sub specie æternitatis* ("from the perspective of eternity"). But it's important to understand that this very different "seeing" or "considering" presupposes a spiritual *metanoia* ("conversion"), without which we would always remain within the restricted confines of the thinking subject.

Esotericism and the risk of pride

BB: As far as esotericism is concerned, don't you find that, often, to think of espousing such a point of view endows a layman or, if you'll pardon the expression, a "non-specialist," with immeasurable pride, hence this Christian accusation of luciferian Gnosticism?

AF: You raise a fundamental problem here, because "esotericists" are often accused of pride, but in truth this accusation is only levelled at false esotericists, not the real thing. The false esotericists are those who, let's be clear, think they're special and believe, as the popular saying goes, "that their egg has two yolks." Sometimes this presumption is fueled by special "psychic faculties," which may have been acquired through certain practices. As a result, these people end up overestimating themselves to the point of feeling like a god on earth. In reality, true esotericists never set themselves up as a new Prometheus; rather, the path they travel makes them ever more humble and ever more eager not to appear and to hide from the world.

BB: But then why does this misunderstanding exist, even when referring to the most authentic esotericism?

AF: I would say that this is especially true of the most suspicious and closed-minded Christians, who do not accept that there can be anything beyond the control of the Magisterium. In other cultures and spiritual traditions, the question doesn't even arise.

BB: Do you have any examples?

AF: Here, esotericists are confused with magicians, mediums, and sorcerers, and esoteric practices with the manufacture of potions and amulets, whereas these are very different realities, which do not even remotely resemble each other, and even if in certain so-called esoteric bookshops one can find all these elements nicely mixed and made interchangeable—from cartomancy to René Guénon. What's more, Christians all too often equate esotericism with the Gnostic heresy or, worse still, Satanism. Elsewhere—in India, Asia or Africa—esotericism is not at issue, as there isn't even a word to define it. In these places, no one would dream of calling a shaman an arrogant, heaven-defying, conceited or a dangerous heretic who "consorts with demons" or hell. These are "our" categories, by which I mean the categories of we Westerners and Europeans, which have no universal character.

BB: Would you say that the accusation of ὕβρις (hubris) for defining the arrogance and pride of certain individuals and certain forms of "esoteric" thought is exaggerated or erroneous?

AF: I'd say that if it addresses true esotericism, it's fictitious, invented. On the other hand, there's no doubt that pride is a real fact, and a capital vice. And this "vice" can afflict anyone, even a Pope... Let's just say that certain ideas or doctrines can fuel disproportionate attitudes, or even ethically questionable behavior. But then, we're dealing with already corrupted esoteric doctrines, or their misinterpretations.

BB: And how do we recognize them?

AF: I would say, in general, by the bad fruits they produce. If the source is pure, participation in it can only generate good fruit in terms of true spirituality, knowledge, and human wisdom. Where unbalanced, or at any rate out-of-step, attitudes appear, they are most probably counterfeit, or pure and simple mental delusions.

Esotericism and humility

BB: So, as you said, it's not so much the content itself that's of primary importance, but the effects it produces on the individual who discovers it.

AF: That's right. I'm not denying that the content is important; I'm just saying that, in the end, what matters is what you get out of it for yourself and for your own spiritual growth. Growth: in the sense of the harmonious and integral development of the person, and as an awareness of the limits of the "I." I call this awareness "humility." The further we advance along the path of knowledge (esotericism-gnosis), the further the ego recedes, until it disappears, as in the previously mentioned example of John the Baptist.

BB: But why should esotericism be a privileged path?

AF: In reality, it's just a path prepared for those who can walk it.

BB: But doesn't all this "knowledge" run the risk of creating a kind of cognitive short-circuit in the minds of those who assume it without precaution and, above all, without adequate prior preparation?

AF: Absolutely! This is why "cognitive humility" is important, because only this humility of mind can save us from braininess and intellectualism as ends in themselves, a condition that afflicts many of today's alleged "esoterists." Stockpiling "esoteric doctrines" in one's brain simply out of curiosity makes no sense, and is a completely pointless and dangerous exercise for one's own mental equilibrium. It's quite another to deal with esotericism for reasons of study, or even for a genuine and ardent desire for knowledge. But it's precisely in this second and third hypothesis that a good dose of cognitive humility is required, not least because it's an extremely magmatic subject we're talking about, requiring more introspection and creative intuition than rationality and reasoning. The mind that has reached a certain point should know where to stop.

BB: A cautious attitude wouldn't hurt either.

AF: Of course. A truly scientific attitude must always be guided by caution. Precisely from a scientific point of view, it's a serious mistake to espouse an exclusive thesis, or to mock anyone who puts forward a different or opposing thesis. The great philosophers have never done this, and have always endeavored to understand (*intelligere*, as the Latins would say) before judging. And this should also be the rule for anyone who applies themselves to the study of esotericism.

Erudite esotericism and arrogance?

BB: Erudition as a form of arrogance…

AF: Yes, sometimes. We tend to get too attached to our theses or interpretations, sometimes under the illusion that we've discovered them. Mind you, this is a problem that also concerns theologians: even they tend to get too attached to their conclusions. Here, however, the ecclesiastical magisterium intervenes to monitor, control, and guide the theologian's opinions back onto the straight and narrow path of orthodoxy. When it comes to esotericism, there has never been a controlling body, a guardianship authority... or, rather, there never was until René Guénon appeared on the scene (laughs).

BB: Guénon, the guardian of esoteric orthodoxy!

AF: Yes, and, believe me, we really needed someone like him, considering how much the occultism of the 19th century had discredited true esotericism.

BB: And yet, even Guénon is accused of presumption.

AF: However, I believe that this accusation is completely unfounded. Guénon was an extremely humble person—those who knew him personally testify to this, and his letters also tell us of a very prudent and wise man. On the other hand, if this were not the case, his perspicacity, his intelligence, his ability to penetrate the most difficult truths—qualities which literally "found a school"—could not be explained. No esoterologist or "esotericist"—given that some of the latter are still alive—seems to be able to do without Guénon. He is a virtually infallible compass, and without his teachings, who knows how much nonsense we ourselves might have said about esotericism in these interviews.

BB: I see you're not denying the Guénonian heritage, and there would be no reason to do so. So, you're saying that humility can preserve the esotericist from error, as well as the esoterologist?

Humility as a criterion

AF: Of course, not always. Being humble is not enough to avoid making mistakes. However, humility is closely linked to truth. There is no truth without humility, as Saint Augustine even said somewhere: "It is pride that has transformed angels into demons. It is humility that makes men equal to angels."[2] Above all, there is no true intelligence without humility, and there can be no doubt that the measure of knowledge depends in some way on the degree of humility. Only in this dependence is knowledge the prescience and understanding of gnosis.

BB: Concerning Guénon, his humility is unquestionable, and his refusal to position himself as a master and take on disciples confirms this, if it were necessary. However, his professorial side, categorical to the point of a certain mathematization of ideas, has two faces: one seems to distance him from an esotericism and a less conceptual or supra-logical metaphysics, which may be a cause of reductionism for some; the other is that this constructed, rational language enabled many to hear him and, in Borella's words, to restore, in the West at least, the possibility of a sacred intellectuality, which has been salutary for many.

AF: Indeed, Guénon addressed an audience of educated and often highly educated readers, and spoke to them in the language of a rigorous philosopher, in the sense that his speculative subjectivity never took precedence over his "spiritual persona," placed at the service of tradition. If we take a close look at his writings as a whole, I think we can safely say that he confined himself to drawing a kind of

---

[2] In substance, it seems, see sermon 123.

"boundary" between what is traditional and what is not. His "system," then, is not an impenetrable monolith, but rather a tree with a thousand branches. If we think of the number of different points of view that have branched off from his discourse—from the "philosopher-mystic" Schuon to the "neopagan" Evola—we can agree that it was an "open system," not a closed one as some readers may have imagined.

BB: And what about the other "masters" of esotericism? Were any of them presumptuous?

AF: So you mean the "bogus teachers"! (laughs). By way of example, I'd just like to mention Giordano Bruno who, with his impetuous nature, had some notable points of presumption that he never seems to have managed to dilute or correct. In Marsilio Ficino and even more so in Pico della Mirandola, these personalist and capricious excesses are not felt, or are felt much less. It's no coincidence that Giordano Bruno's interest and fame grew precisely with the Enlightenment, and that his work influenced the prince of rationalist philosophers, Descartes.

BB: And our contemporaries?

AF: Still by way of example, I would say that Arturo Reghini was a rather "arrogant" and conceited esotericist. As a scholar, he was excellent, but as a man, he had serious limitations. Some of his critical and hypercritical excesses towards Christianity are, spiritually speaking, unspeakably ungenerous and not at all "esoteric." A Julius Evola, who was at one time quite friendly with him, and in many respects also resembled him, was ultimately more "traditional" than he was—which is saying a lot!

BB: Among the authors who have drawn inspiration from René Guénon's work, are there any you would describe as arrogant?

AF: I wouldn't say arrogant, except for some of his admirers who idolized him to the point of disfiguring his image and betraying his work. The latter often appropriated the knowledge they received and used it as a bludgeon against anyone who didn't think like them. In this respect, Evola spoke of an "intransigent Guénonian scholasticism,"[3] but it's not easy to be a disciple when the master is so much superior to us. Being a disciple is an art that implies the ability to change, to transform oneself, to acquire one's own autonomous self, and unfortunately not everyone is capable of this.

BB: I understand you're not naming names; wouldn't it be arrogant to call others that? But perhaps you could mention the names of those who weren't?

AF: Certainly: Titus Burckhardt (1908–1984) and Ananda Kentish Coomaraswamy (1877–1947), who never pontificated once in their lives, and always demonstrated great humility and wisdom. In them, we perceive no intrusion or domination of the ego. On the other hand, the most obvious signs of humility are gentleness, modesty, and benevolence, qualities in which the two good scholars excelled.

BB: Pope Francis often speaks of pride as the most dangerous attitude for the life of a Christian, and the Doctors of the Church have always feared "spiritual pride"...

---

[3] In *Quaderni di testi evoliani* n. 19 (Roma: Fondazione Julius Evola, 2001).

AF: And they were right, even if calling a one-sided feeling of excessive self-esteem "spiritual" is a theological and anthropological oxymoron. It would be better to speak of anti-spiritual pride. In any case, the Church uses this expression to define a person who claims to want to elevate himself above God, who boasts, not only of his works as if they were only his own, but also of presumed spiritual privileges.

BB: It's a risk we dread, especially when we've embarked on a spiritual path. Certain "conquests" can strengthen the ego rather than weaken it...

AF: And the risk is all the greater if the person's demands and expectations are very high, as can be the case for those who follow an "esoteric" path. In fact, this "path" can lead to an initial strengthening of the ego. Hence the need for a master or "spiritual father," without whom, it should be firmly stated, you won't get very far, unless you have special help from on high.

BB: On the other hand, recognizing the need for a spiritual master is already an act of humility.

AF: Absolutely! If things were seen from this angle, many a blunder and misjudgment would be avoided. Of course, then we have to beware of "false prophets" and "false teachers," and in the esoteric field—but we should say "pseudo-esoteric"—the risk is very high.

BB: Knowing how to recognize them, in a word discernment,[4] isn't that also a fact of "humility"?

---

[4] See P. Bovati, "Alla ricerca del profeta. II. Criteri per discernere i veri profeti," *Rivista del Clero* 67 (1986), 179.

AF: Well, let's say it has even more to do with insight: "Be ye therefore wise as serpents, and simple as doves." (Matt. 10:16) A sense of proportion (Schuon's definition of humility), or being aware of one's limits, isn't it precisely a question of "prudence"? Prudence is inseparable from humility, while imprudence is an act of pride.

BB: Finally, in this interview, we didn't talk about *your own* "cognitive humility," as "proclaimed" by Carlo Gambescia. But how could that simply be possible? Humility, in general and as a spiritual quality, is far more precious.

AF: Whether or not my intellectual attitude has always accompanied my esoteric studies is of far less importance. It was important to recall here the importance of a virtue which not only must characterize the student of any discipline, but which is at the root of any spiritual itinerary, and without which the path, any path, immediately stops or forks. This applies all the more to the narrow path of esotericism.

Chapter 17
What is Esotericism?

After such a panorama of this question, it was absolutely necessary to attempt this exercise of defining esotericism. That's the aim of this final interview.

BB: We have reviewed a considerable number of esotericists and esoterisms. We have compared esotericism with science, religion, and metaphysics. We've studied the esotericism of many religions across space and time. I propose now that we attempt a synthetic definition of esotericism.

AF: A definition is a delimitation of conceptual boundaries. A concept, in turn, is a defined thought, ideally configured and formulable. With definitions and concepts, then, we are in the realm of human words, whereas to frame esotericism, which is something in the world but not of the world (John 17:14), we need to go beyond what can be said.

BB: To the question: "What is esotericism?" should the answer be silence?

Esotericism, towards a definition

AF: That would actually be a good way of saying goodbye, in an esoteric way (laughs). Let's just say that when faced with certain questions, we should behave like Jesus in the episode of the adulterous woman:[1] bend down and start

---

[1] John 8:1–11.

writing on the ground with one's finger. But we are very few for such a gesture, which belongs to the greatness of a Master and a God.

BB: And so for the rest of us who are, at best, dwarfs on the shoulders of giants, there's still room for words; words that aren't definitive, but certainly conclusive in relation to what we've said so far.

AF: Yes, at this stage, we must at least summarize. We've started by explaining the etymological meaning of the word "esotericism," and we've outlined its historical, anthropological, cultural, and spiritual context. Anyone who reads us and wasn't informed at least learned something more about the genealogy of the word, its evolution, and the different realities to which it's linked. We've also seen how it "resonates," so to speak, in each of us in a different way, and how it has become a "magic" word, one that evokes a mysterious and intangible reality. Hence, on the one hand, its great "suggestive power" and, on the other, the discredit that continues to weigh on the word and doesn't seem easy to shake off.

BB: Can you explain the "suggestive power" of this word?

AF: It confirms the existence of a hidden reality, hidden from our sight and senses, even ignored because it is disguised or deliberately concealed. It's this aura of mystery that surrounds it that makes it fascinating, and, at the same time, it's this secrecy that discredits it. All the perplexities or, on the contrary, all the enthusiasms that such a word arouses are fostered precisely by its historical and semantic indeterminacy.

BB: So, in your opinion, our attempt at clarification won't change this state of affairs either?

AF: No, I really don't think it will change anything! There will always be those who identify esotericism with a load of nonsense, and those who, on the contrary, think of it as another science, as a borderline science, as total knowledge inaccessible to most, and as a mystery. And even if someone more qualified than ourselves were to attempt to arbitrate this insoluble dispute, he or she would not succeed, and would at best be forced to suspend all judgment.

BB: Perhaps we decided to take the whole affair seriously, but a little too late, as the word had already fallen into the realm of equivocation.

AF: I believe that esoterology in the 20th century has made an important contribution in terms of historical elucidation, but there is an extra-documentary and extra-historical dimension that continues and will always continue to elude us. The esoterologist must not be very different from a theologian who knows that to understand what he's dealing with, he must first "believe." For this reason, in my opinion, the best esoterologists are those who take esotericism very seriously and are animated, so to speak, by a spirit of almost religious fervor.

BB: Can you name a few?

Some current or contemporary esoterologists

AF: C.G. Jung (1875–1961) was, in my opinion, an excellent esoterologist, perhaps among the best and most competent. The pages he wrote on this subject are extraordinarily rich and inspiring. And I won't go into the substance of the psychological or psychoanalytical framework he gave to the theme, which, from my point of view, is profoundly wrong, as well as—metaphysically and spiritually—unacceptable. It is the framework of competence and seriousness he has given to the subject that is commendable and admirable. Great mythographers such as K. Kerényi (1897–1973), J. Campbell (1904–1987), and J. Hillman (1926–2011) would not have existed without him. And if this is the case, then for Mircea Eliade the encounter with Jung was also crucial to the crystallization of his thought and the construction of his lexicon.

BB: Any other names?

AF: Well, in the first place, I would mention the Roman Julius Evola (1898–1974) and, secondly, the Turin-born Elemire Zolla (1926–2002). Both, in their early days, were conditioned by opposing ideological constructs of German origin, Evola by the *Conservative Revolution* and Zolla by the *Frankfurter Schule.* But both treated the theme of esotericism in a comprehensive way, offering a vast and complete panorama. Obviously, from my point of view, some of their interpretations remain debatable; I would define them more as "a-religious" than supra-religious, but in Europe and the world, there has been no one else on their level, and this must be honestly acknowledged.

BB: And René Guénon? He could also be considered an esoterologue, don't you think?

AF: Of course. But Guénon investigated esotericism *from the inside* and, thus, with more penetrating capacity than all the others, including Jung, Evola, and Zolla.

BB: And nowadays? Is there anyone alive equal to these greats?

AF: In France there is the École Pratique des Hautes Études, and there are worthy scholars like Jean-Pierre Brach and Jean-Pierre Laurant whom I've already mentioned. Perhaps I could add the Austrian Hans Thomas Hakl,[2] who has developed exceptional expertise on the subject and possesses perhaps one of the world's finest and richest libraries in this domain; I believe it is even superior to that compiled by Umberto Eco.

BB: There are a lot of them in Italy, I think.

AF: Among the most important and authoritative scholars in Italy, I will mention Alessandro Grossato, Nuccio D'Anna, Claudio Lanzi, and Dario Chiloli. The truth is, there are not many other eminent people in the field of esotericism, but there are talented scholars who don't write and about whom practically nothing is known. I myself have met and known many of them in the course of my life.

BB: Let's just say that to understand something you have to read and gather a lot of information, and it's not easy to find the material. In your opinion, what are the minimum requirements for a neophyte?

AF: I would say that erudition is *too much*, and an esoteric organization is *too little*—the member only accessing what is strictly, or very strictly, necessary to follow the proposed path. As far as I'm concerned, the only things that count are aptitude, temperament, virtue, vocation, patience, constancy, commitment and, in short, all those human and intellectual qualities that constitute the necessary and indispensable prerequisites.

---

[2] A law graduate (University of Graz, 1970), he established the Ansata-Verlag publishing house, specializing in esotericism, and founded the esoteric and academic journal *Gnostika*, of which he is still co-director.

BB: What then would be the definition of esotericism that could be given to this neophyte, endowed with these qualities and therefore "capable of understanding"?

Esotericism, the way of the invisible

AF: Well, we could tell him that esotericism is that path which will familiarize him with the invisible or, we could say, with the Soul. We could also tell him that it's the experience of the Soul that awaits him; an anticipation of what we experience in death and after death. And perhaps telling him this might also dissuade him from attempting this path, which is certainly not the easiest route to well-being or happiness, as some innocent or naive people might imagine.

BB: Let's say: a path that opens the doors to perception and the invisible?

AF: Yes, a path that amplifies perceptions beyond matter and beyond the visible; that makes us more capable of attention and sharpens the intelligence, making it capable of true understanding. Esotericism takes us beyond what Pliny the Elder called the *linea summae tenuitatis*, the "thinnest" line that separates the visible from the invisible.[3]

BB: And once this "line" has been crossed, what happens to the esotericist?

AF: Where the outside and the inside coincide, where there is no longer an inside and an outside, one is reborn and liberated from the illusions of this world. At this point, the esotericist can become a simple, essential, and pure creature, like Buddha and Laozi.

---

[3] Cf. *Naturalis Historia*, Liber xxxv, 81–83.

BB: With these names, we're back to the idea of a path reserved for a privileged few.

AF: Well, there's no denying that there are few, or very few, people with the right aptitude for this Way. But deep down, I don't think it's such a difficult concept to accept. Geniuses have always existed in every field, and there's no reason why they shouldn't also exist in the spiritual realm. Once it's been accepted that such people exist, all that's needed is for Providence to provide them with the means in keeping with their talents—let's say, the means best suited to their "spiritual needs."

BB: If I'm not mistaken, Guénon was the representative of a contemplative "priestly esotericism." Others, like Evola for example, spoke of an esotericism aimed at the warrior class, not subordinate to, but an alternative to priestly esotericism. Hence, a certain disagreement between the two. On the other hand, we know that there was also an esotericism adapted to the artisan class and even for those who, still Hindus, would define themselves as "outcasts"—I'm thinking of tantrism as the "way of the left hand" and other similar paths. Whatever the vision of Guénon or Evola, aren't all these differences between the various esotericisms factual proof of a non-unitary reality?

Esotericism: the one and the many

AF: I could answer by saying that the desire for truth animates all men in general, and that it is right that each person should be granted his or her own Way. Esotericism is a plural reality, there's no doubt about it. There is a priestly art, a prophetic art, a royal art, a craft art, a worker's art, and so on. These are all arts appropriate to the nature of the human beings who practice them. As for esotericism, the problem is that there are no longer any schools or organizations that teach such arts, nor any teachers who transmit them adequately! Esotericism seems to have become an object of historical study, an intellectual speculation, a literary fact, a leisure activity, a hobby, an escape, even an escape from reality.

BB: Is esotericism really in such bad shape? When you see "personal growth," which is the very opposite of esotericism, taking shelter under the banner of esotericism, you'd think so. What, then, is the fundamental and discriminating feature of true esotericism?

AF: In the most extreme synthesis, I would say that the distinguishing trait is the polarized tension between the visible and the invisible; the ability to transform flesh into spirit and spirit into flesh. This finality belongs to all authentic esotericism. Anything that betrays or denies this polarity is a false esotericism, a deviated esotericism, or a non-esotericism.

BB: Materialism and spiritism shift away from this necessary polarization.

AF: Absolutely. If you think about it, these two positions are mirrorlike and, in appearance only, antithetical. And it's no coincidence that both are deviations induced by erroneous religious beliefs. The materialist rejects the afterlife because of an overestimation of matter; the spiritualist focuses on the afterlife because of an underestimation of matter. As for the idealist, he believes that all reality can be attributed to thought, and denies both matter and spirit. These conceptions inevitably lead to unrealism, and can herald deceptive "escapes from reality" or generate forms of alienation.

BB: In fact, a well-understood doctrine of the resurrection of the flesh, as we know it in Christianity, resolves by integration the artificial separation between spirit and matter.

AF: This is true, even if Christians themselves sometimes seem to forget it. In this respect, what Gustav Meyrink wrote in his famous esoteric novel *The White Dominican* comes to mind: "The most profound secret of all secrets, the most hidden mystery of all mysteries, is the alchemical transformation of the . . . body."[4] The esotericist understands that reality is not made up of opposites, but of complementarities, and attempts to achieve their synthesis within himself. In this sense, esotericism is based on a broader, less oxymoronic conception of reality. One of the causes of materialism and mass atheism has been the suppression of the "in-between world," not only by science, but also by religion. In this sense, esotericism is more scientific than science and more religious than popular religion, because its idea of an integral reality that includes invisible, but very real and testable worlds, doesn't require the logical and theoretical leaps that science actually demands, or religion's over-separation of this life from the other. The increase in psychiatric pathologies and mental disorders is the fatal consequence of a truncated conception of reality and a spiritual life that is soulless or detached from reality. Obviously, this is not a criticism of religion, but of a certain sociological or spiritualist conception of religion; likewise, it is not a criticism of science, but of scientific materialism and scientism.

4 Trans. M. Mitchell (Sawtry, UK: Dedalus, 1994), 112.

Esotericism: mediating between science and religion?

BB: Thus the esoteric perspective could also have the task of encouraging religion and science not to limit their respective domains too much, and to consider the possibility of other cognitive paths and other "research methods," as essentially taught by Plato and Aristotle.

AF: Yes, I sincerely think so. Esotericism, if taken seriously, could have a mediating function between religion and science. A third term of comparison capable of mitigating and balancing these unilateralisms.

BB: Could this be the mission of speculative esotericism in the 21st century?

AF: More than speculative esotericism, I would speak of the worldview associated with its doctrines. There is, of course, a risk that esotericism will lose its innermost, truest dimension and, in short, its true "initiatory" and spiritual function. But, having reached this point, we must try to do something to save what can be saved, and esotericism could indeed lend a helping hand.

BB: Let's hope that this book will be useful in this very sense!

AF: Yes, I hope so with all my heart, even if I don't believe it.

BB: Let's not put limits on Divine Providence!

AF: No, let's not, God forbid! (laughs).

BB: Well, I think we've come to the end of this last interview. Is there anything else you'd like to add?

AF: Yes, I would just like to add that it was an honor and a pleasure to have you as my interlocutor for this interview and to thank you for your always intelligent, polite, punctual, and pressing questions, which enabled me to express my thoughts freely and without censorship. I also hope that I haven't bored the reader and that I've provided some useful food for thought.

BB: I'd like to thank you and ask you to conclude with a quote from a serious and qualified representative of authentic esotericism.

ALF: Very well, then I'll end with these words from Plotinus from his famous book *The Enneads*:

> The teaching comes only to show the way and the journey, but the vision will come to him who wants to see. (VI, 9, 4)

Appendix

The Tree of Sephiroth

The process of principial substantialization
according to the symbolism of the Kabbalah

"On high," *Keter* is the infinite Receptivity of *Binah*
by virtue of which God reveals Himself; 'below' he is
the cosmic Receptivity of *Malkhuth*, which concret-
izes itself into creative substance.

In other words, what is pure Receptivity in *Binah*, and creative contraction in *Din*, becomes cosmic Vacuity in *Hod* and ends up being elusive and causal Substance in *Malkhuth*.

"This process of principal 'substantialization' has its positive point of departure in *Hokhmah*, whose luminous fullness is manifested by *Hesed*, to receive from *Tifereth* its universal form and manifest itself as the 'Life of worlds,' the Life which *Yesod* communicates to *Malkhuth*, Substance." (Leo Schaya, *The Universal Meaning of the Kabbalah*, 59)

Afterword

Readers of this book will easily realize that, despite its title, this is not a new version of "Esotericism for Dummies." More than an academic or other type of definition, difficult to formulate and often of illusory benefit (see the last chapter), *Esotericism for Everyone* actually offers the means for *discernment* concerning esotericism, its nature, and its functions.

Without ignoring the historical dimension of the subject, or the idiosyncrasies of a number of more or less famous authors in the field under consideration, this discernment is intended above all to be of a spiritual nature, since it deals with esotericism as an *approach*, present in the most diverse horizons, universal in this sense, but nevertheless religiously and culturally differentiated according to varied contexts.

The dialogue form chosen here lends the text a welcome flexibility, enabling it to move smoothly between different registers—historical, thematic, autobiographical, etc. The seventeen chapters are often well-informed, avoiding the twin pitfalls of either overwhelming erudition or a false quest for exhaustiveness, and offer a panorama of esotericism marked by a central—but not exclusive—reference to Christianity on the one hand, and to the work of René Guénon on the other.

While the book's dominant perspective is indeed Christian, and even distinctly Catholic, it courageously attempts to distinguish between the two, shedding light on the ways in which a "Christian esotericism" can manifest itself, and consequently evoking its relationship to common religion, or comparing its possible characteristics with those of other forms of esotericism linked to different traditional beliefs. The awareness of the existence, at least until the 4th century, of "secret traditions" within early Christianity, stressed—following certain Greek Fathers—by historians as different as A. Daniélou, J. Jeremias, or G. G. Stroumsa, ends up supporting the idea that there is no *a priori* incompatibility between esotericism and the Christian message, contrary to an all too widespread opinion recently contested by the Rev. Jérôme Rousse-Lacordaire, O.P.

Without wishing to go into details that have no place in a simple afterword, and without concealing the almost total absence of documentary evidence to establish the actual historical continuity of such traditions, nor the exact nature of the techniques or means used in this context (on which ancient authors remained almost mute), it seems that the properly gnoseological aspect, relating therefore to "spiritual knowledge," is predominant. This kind of "knowledge" is supposed to be based more on lived assimilation than on scholarly accumulation, and above all on suprarational intuition, already dear to Aristotle, the Neoplatonists, and the Church Fathers. This is a possible link with other confessional approaches, such as Indian metaphysics, as well as with the "traditional" approach advocated in his time by René Guénon.

It should also be noted that the strong revival of interest in the question of "divinization" within Latin Christianity since the late 1930s is in fact closely linked to this doctrine of the "transcendent intellect" and its rediscovery under the influence of certain theologians of the Russian Orthodox *diaspora*, particularly in France. The central idea here is that of "knowledge by connaturality," which is not only specu-

lative in the abstract sense, but also practical, in that it aims
to consummate the "savory" union (as one knows, "sapid-
ity" and "wisdom" have the same root) that is a gracious gift
of the Spirit to our spirit. For some years now, the contemporary revival of studies on the representatives of the medieval mystical current known as "Rheno-Flemish" has
confirmed the importance of this supra-discursive "infused
intellectual contemplation," to use the language of certain
scholastics, which the Dominican theologian E.-P. Noël
had already emphasized a few years before the Great War (a
fact that is sufficiently exceptional at this date in France to
be well worth noting), in the annotation accompanying his
Parisian edition of the works of J. Tauler.

The confluence of ontology and knowledge—in other
words, the synthesis between the activity of the intellect,
that of the will at the ascetic-moral level, and the interven-
tion of divine grace—is the primary condition for the concrete demand for spiritual transformation that naturally lies
at the heart of the Christian approach, and that also animates—*mutatis mutandis*—the trajectory of other faith-
based approaches. In times that ignore the conceptual regis-
ter or vocabulary of "esotericism" *per se*, the latter can be
hidden behind the exercise of that practical, transforming
virtue attributed to contemplation, or focused on certain
discreet ritual means rather than on the doctrinal content
they underpin, which is, in principle, accessible to all. Such
an emphasis on the secrecy of "techniques" is a constant in
Eastern religions (yoga, Chinese alchemy, etc.) but is also
found, all things being equal, in hesychasm, Jewish kabbalah, or Sufism. An important aspect is also the more or
less explicit claim to unitive contact with divinity obtained
directly *in this life*, a claim already present in Hellenistic

theurgy and Hermeticism, or even—later—in Renaissance Christian kabbalah. By the end of the 15th century, moreover, the alleged similarity between the latter and invocatory "angelic magic" did much to lend credence to the widespread assimilation of religion with magic and Kabbalah. The former is sometimes seen as a "spiritualization" of the latter, and the latter as externalizing the unifying effects of *ascensio mentis* into the cosmic and human order, while Kabbalah itself is said to lead man, by similar means, to a mystical *raptus* and various forms of angelomorphosis.

For complex reasons beyond the scope of these lines, from the end of the 17th century onwards certain tendencies within German-speaking Lutheran Pietism, which were predominantly theosophical (in the Boehmian sense of the word), developed a practice of "inner alchemy" aimed above all at combining Christian devotion, medicine, and transmutation with a view to physical regeneration, which, in this perspective, became confused with deifying union, understood more specifically this time in terms of spiritual healing and bodily rejuvenation. The theme of Christ's Incarnation, combined with that of his growth as an "inner man" (partly inherited from Rheno-Flemish literature), forms the bedrock of this particular form of "Protestant esotericism," rather eclectic on the doctrinal level (like that of many pietistic circles), which was subsequently often labelled "Rosicrucian" or "Illuminist" with little historical justification, even when applied in a Masonic context, where it became widespread especially after 1740.

As for later occultism (the term dates back to the 19th century), it fostered the emergence of an "esoteric" sociability and the creation of specialized salons, bookshops, magazines and almanacs, emphasized the importance of gender and the role of women, distanced itself from established religions, emphasized the importance of the body and sexuality, then refocused its perspectives on the inner "Self" and the study of psychology or different states of consciousness (in parallel with the "psychic studies" conducted by William James or F.W.H. Myers).

We also read with interest the rather personal suggestions contained in the chapters devoted to the relationship between esotericism and science, mysticism or metaphysics, which attempt to reconcile the author's views with the requirements of a certain religious semantics and the perspectives traced out on these themes by René Guénon. For, let us repeat, it is indeed an assent, a point of view (almost in the sense of a Hindu *darshan*), an "esoteric gaze" (to quote Jean-Pierre Laurant) that is at stake here, rather than an attempt at an objective, fixed definition. As voiced in these pages, esotericism seems above all to mobilize a multiplicity of fine, highly personal understandings, corresponding to as many orientations proper to the spiritual life.

JEAN-PIERRE BRACH

About the Authors

BRUNO BÉRARD (1958–), PhD ("Religions and Systems of Thought," École pratique des hautes études—Sorbonne) is the author of metaphysical essays and studies (some now translated and published in the United States and Italy). He is the editor of several collective books, and has also published works on metaphysics by other authors.

ALDO LA FATA (1964–) is an orientalist and historian of religions with a special interest in Christian esotericism and the esoteric tradition. For many years he worked under Silvano Panunzio as editor-in-chief of the universal studies journal *Metapolitica*, and currently heads the journal *Il Corriere Metapolitico*. He is the author, translator, and editor of numerous books.